I0129731

The End of the Middle

Farid Tabarki

The End of the Middle

What a Society of Extremes Means for People, Politics and Business

Warden Press

© 2017 Farid Tabarki

ISBN:
Paperback: 978-94-92004-42-0
E-book (Epub): 978-94-92004-43-7
E-book (Kindle): 978-94-92004-44-4

Original title: *Het einde van het midden. Wat een maatschappij van extremen betekent voor mens, bedrijf en overheid* (Amsterdam: Business Contact, 2016). Translated from the Dutch by Mark Baker.

Research and text contribution: Rindert de Groot, Amsterdam
Cover design: Pankra, Den Haag
Lay-out and DTP: Bert Holtkamp, Groningen
Photo author: Binh Tran, Amsterdam

This edition published by Warden Press, Amsterdam.
All rights reserved. No part of this publication may be reproduced, stored in a retrieval system, or transmitted in any form or by any means, electronic, mechanical, photocopying, recording or otherwise without the prior written permission of the publisher.

Table of Contents

Foreword

Standing in the middle of the road is very dangerous:
you get knocked down by traffic from both sides.
Margaret Thatcher

There's a cool video on YouTube of a boy tipping a pan of boiling water off the balcony of a seventh-floor flat. But no one gets hurt: before the water can hit the ground, it's turned to snow. We are in Siberia, and the song 'Troika' by Dutch poet and cabaret artist Doctorandus P is comes to mind: 'We're driving our troika through the forests vast and old / It's thirty below zero, it is winter and quite cold.' Between the seventh floor and the ground, the water goes through a 'phase transition', changing from a liquid to a solid. The transparent liquid becomes a white powder.

The society in which we live is also going through such a phase transition, but the other way around. Clearly defined structures are making way for a new order that will allow us human beings to move much more freely. A rigid form is giving way to fluidity.

Luckily, unlike the unfortunate characters in Doctorandus P's cruel song, who get tossed out one by one to keep the pursuing pack of hungry wolves at bay, when I travelled through Siberia it wasn't in a troika. I used a more modern (yet also timeless) mode of transport: the deservedly legendary Trans-Siberian Railway. The journey takes forever. To quote the song again, 'While the wolves devour me my mind wanders astray / Yes, Omsk is a lovely town, but just too far away'. During the endless ride, you get to know your fellow passengers pretty well. The *konduktorska* serves tea from a samovar, but to liven up the cultural exchange a little more you take some vodka along too. If you didn't, someone in your compartment certainly will have.

All the way into Siberia, computers and the connections between them are rearranging society. To use my analogy: society is being transformed into a liquid. These developments are pumping so much energy into our system that we sense the vibration all around us. In relation to the organisation of people and knowledge, the traditional, rigid forms of institutions and organisations are increasingly making way for the more liquid, transparent nature of the network. This is exactly what molecules do when they warm up.

The industrial age of Henry Ford and Frederick Taylor with their conveyor belts and rigidly planned companies, the leading form of (commercial) organisation throughout the twentieth century, from the USA to the Soviet Union, is over, for good. We will have to come out of our offices and (literal and figurative) cubicles and break our habit of thinking in hierarchies.

The great thing about the liquid society – also referred to by Polish-British sociologist and philosopher Zygmunt Bauman as 'liquid modernity', is that you don't have to be a Ford or a Taylor to change the world. Anyone can do it, from behind his or her computer and within his or her own network. This has already led to companies with twelve employees being valued in the billions (like Instagram) and turning entire sectors upside down thanks to a flexible platform (like Airbnb in the hotel sector and Uber for taxis). The establishment of politics and government are also slowly starting to thaw: citizens and *the powers that be* are now just one click away from one another and are finding one another with ever greater ease.

For a long time, our society was like a pyramid: made out of stone, with a hierarchical structure and a clear stratification into top, middle and bottom. In the liquid society, the pyramid is melting, while its layers are dissolving and joining together.

I am interested in what this liquid society means for the people who traditionally occupy the middle: the travel agent, the shopkeeper, the hotelier – but also the civil servant, the manager and the teacher. The organisations and institutions in the middle are also feeling the force of these changes: from big players in manufacturing to national governments.

One thing becomes very clear as you sit in that Russian train, watching all those decaying industrial sites slide by: all institutions come to an end. Nothing lasts forever. Again in Bauman's words: the only certainty is uncertainty.

One branch of the Trans-Siberian Railway ends in China, where 'may you live in interesting times' is a well-known curse. I see this a bit differently: even though it can be very tiring to have to keep on reinventing yourself, it is also fascinating. And with sufficient inspiration from a good book, a journey and good conversation – whether over a cup of tea or a glass of vodka – it can be a hugely enjoyable trip.
Na zdorovie.

1

A liquid revolution

What the Pope and Lady Gaga can teach us about decentralisation and transparency

In this chapter, I start off in Rome. The Pope and Lady Gaga are both superstars, and turn out to be quite similar in some unexpected ways. I use the terms 'radical decentralisation' and 'radical transparency' and show how these developments are threatening the existence of the middle, or at least forcing it to reinvent itself. Smart platforms are taking the place of the intermediaries of old, and different roles are being combined. Consumers are becoming prosumers; guests are becoming hoteliers. These developments, driven by social and technological changes, are leading to a liquid society. They are so far-reaching we can see them as a revolution.

A revolution is not a trail of roses. A revolution is a fight to the death between the future and the past.

Fidel Castro

Crushed by a giant

I was staring eternity in the face: above me the enormous dome, clearly intended to make all those who gaze up at it feel small. The architect succeeded in his plan. TV ES PETRVS ET SVPER HANC PETRAM AEDIFICABO ECCLESIAM MEAM. TIBI DABO CLAVES REGNI CAELORUM I read, while slowly rotating – 'You are Peter and upon this rock I shall build my Church. To you I give the keys to the Kingdom of Heaven.' Below the dome is the main altar with the bronze baldachin, and below this the grave of Saint Peter. It was not until the last century (during World War II) that it was discovered that Peter is in fact buried here, far below the surface, at the level of the necropolis. It took several centuries to prove that the seven architects of this giant church, including Bernini and Michelangelo, who rebuilt it during the Renaissance, were right when they placed their enormous letters around the dome – at least as far as the first sentence is concerned.

Saint Peter's Basilica made me nauseated, partly from spinning round to read the text, partly because of the building's intimidating and megalomaniac proportions. As a homage to the unbridled power and wealth of one of the oldest organisations in the world, it is hard to digest. Humanity's desire for eternal life is as durable as the stone in apostle Peter's name. I quickly left the Basilica, emerging into the immenseness of Bernini's square, from where the Pope blesses the city and the world every Easter. Here, I still

felt the weight of the World's Church – true, there was no longer a dome that could come crashing down about my ears;
but there were still the heavens. During this trip, I started to
think about change – a thought-process stimulated all the
more when you are literally and metaphorically on the move.

The Pope starts a revolution

Under the stewardship of the new pontiff, Francis, the Catholic Church is presenting a more modern face to the world.
For example, this Pope uses digital media to get his message
out. Let's take a look at the Holy Father's Twitter account
(@Pontifex), which serves millions of followers in nine
languages. Take two random tweets: '*The Christian who does
not feel that the Virgin Mary is his or her mother is an orphan*'
and '*The Lord always forgives us and walks at our side. We
have to let him do that.*' Not really astonishing statements for
the leader of the Roman Catholic Church, and the same can
be said of the hundreds of other statements this Pope and his
predecessor have made through this medium since February
2012. What is exceptional is the fact that the Pope is Twittering at all. Following politicians, pop stars and regular citizens, the head of the oldest multinational in the world now
has an online presence; we can all re-Tweet his thoughts,
and in so doing make them a tiny bit our own.

  According to publicist Nassim Taleb (author of *The Black
Swan*), the Catholic Church is the most successful organisation ever – not thanks to its centralised hierarchy, but
rather because it is made up of small units. Taleb stated in an
interview that this is 'because the Pope doesn't do anything
except appear on TV. All the decisions are taken at lower
levels. If the Pope ever does take a decision, it always goes
wrong.'[1] Taleb sees this as a good lesson for multinationals,
which continue to exist because they enjoy protection from
nation states. 'In a natural situation, large companies would

be doomed to disappear unless they were made up of individual elements. Make way for others, that's the idea behind evolution.'[2]

Taleb makes an interesting point: sometimes it is better to get things done on a smaller scale. Nevertheless, having a global stage can be very important, provided that it's flexible and tailor-made. The Pope is being helped by a smart PR strategy; it's not without reason that Pope Francis is so incredibly popular. He also makes efficient use of the power he wields over the Vatican mini-state. He has been praised for his modernising influence, aimed at transforming the Vatican into a more modern organisation: the traditional power structure has undergone radical surgery, including its finance structures.

Leadership and transparency

Let's take a look at the Vatican Bank – officially known as the Institute for the Works of Religion ('Istituto per le Opere di Religione' in Italian, abbreviated to IOR). In April 2014, more than a year after ascending the throne of St. Peter, the new Pope announced a thorough overhaul of the bank's structure, refusing to even rule out closing it down. The bank's annual report for 2013, published a few months later, did not make for reassuring reading: profits of just 2.9 million Euros, as opposed to 86.6 million the previous year, hit a historic low for this most remarkable of banks. This does not say all that much actually, as the bank didn't publish any annual reports prior to 2012.[3]

A small bank with just 19, 000 account-holders, IOR had a reputation as a money-laundering service for the mafia and shady clerics. For example, Nunzio Scarano was arrested in 2013 for smuggling 20 million Euros from Switzerland to Italy with the aim of avoiding tax. Many others have since been similarly caught. Among the losses for 2013 is a loan of

almost 20 million Euros, written off for a production company belonging to a friend of Tarcisio Bertone, the former
number two in the Vatican under the previous Pope. It probably came as little surprise to Vatican watchers that Bertone
was implicated in financial scandals, as this Cardinal is the
embodiment of the old-style Vatican. Under Benedict XVI,
he was just as inviolable as the dogmatic teachings of the
Church and its many centuries-old institutions. In 2014,
however, there was a big scandal when it was said he was
moving into a stunning four-storey penthouse in Rome.[4] It
has been reported that Pope Francis was furious about Bertone's profligacy. Whether this is true or not the Lord God
only knows, but it is a fact that Bertone has lost his lucrative
job and that Francis is taking a very different approach from
his predecessor, Benedict. For example, the new Pope likes
to eat in the refectory of the guest quarters at Casa Santa
Maria, where he resides. Whereas Benedict was a brilliant
theologian with a love of pomp and circumstance, Francis
demonstrates modesty, a great flair for PR and clear leadership qualities.

In addition to separating the competent sheep from the
corrupt goats, the Pope has done a lot more to bring this
centuries-old multinational in line with the demands of the
age. Next to leadership, transparency is his watchword. And
this is not limited to Twitter and the other activities of the
Church's media branch (the *Pontificium Consilium de Com-
municationibus Socialibus*, as it has been known since 1988).
The economy is also being submitted to greater transparency. The little Vatican Bank is just one example. The newly
established Secretariat for the Economy, headed by Cardinal
Pell, has been charged with making sweeping changes to the
Byzantine structure of the Vatican state finances, replacing
it with a structure more akin to that of a modern state. The
bureaucracy – long known for being rigidly hierarchical – is

being overhauled; alongside transparency, decentralisation is a major goal.

Towards a decentralised, transparent Church

The Vatican exudes monolithic wealth, but in reality the Catholic Church is decentralised when it comes to finance. The finances of Rome are separate from those of the 296 religious orders and 2,846 dioceses, meaning that the Pope's power is not absolute. Taleb, pleading for small, autonomous units, would be satisfied. A global platform should preferably be headed not by a tyrant, but by a leader who is able to inspire the masses, keep his own house in order and keep track of common aims. Francis seems to score a lot higher in relation to this ideal than his predecessor. The media are highly enthusiastic. *The Economist* has called him the first modern Pope, writing: 'Like a great CEO, he has the ability to set a strategic vision, then choose and motivate the right people to make it work. His rapid overhaul of the Vatican's finances is both one of the most unusual case studies in the annals of business and one of the more instructive.' *Fortune* was also impressed, in 2014 putting the Pope at number one in its list of world leaders.

Not unimportantly, these changes are also going down extremely well with the faithful. One of the reasons for this is that the Pope himself sets a good example. His clothes, transportation, accommodation and food: the Pope demonstrates modesty in all of these. In so doing, he stresses the Church's principal duty: to relieve the burden on the poorest, following the example of Saint Francis, whose name he has adopted. Another important factor is the Pope's eloquence. He speaks vividly, on Twitter and elsewhere. According to the *National Catholic Reporter*, Francis has referred to the desire to climb the hierarchical career ladder as 'a form of cancer', and to priests parading in excessively decorated vestments as 'peacocks'. He has referred to 'airport bishops' who jet around the world preaching doctrine while enjoying the good life, as 'little monsters'.[5]

Caring for the disadvantaged is a clear mission, and a business-like approach a clear instruction to the global Church. Emphasising the strength of small units, combined with open dialogue and clear procedures, turns out to be a good way of getting this seized-up, inward-looking mega-institution moving again. The message to bishops and believers alike is in any event clear: it is up to you.

this promising start of Pope Francis' tenure will lead to permanent change remains to be seen. He has in any event expressed contrition and, as any good Catholic will tell you, confession leads to redemption – so who knows.

I will return to Francis and his Church below. But as I don't want this book to turn into an encyclical, I think this would be a good moment to leave the vaulted magnificence of Saint Peter's Basilica for the blue skies above a huge pop concert. I therefore turn to another latter-day superstar: Lady Gaga.

The Queen of Twitter

I haven't followed Lady Gaga's Twitter account for some time now, but I do regularly check how many followers she has. The number in staggering. Her more than 55 million followers put the singer in the top 10 most followed people. In 2015, she earned no less than 60 million dollars, putting her at number 4 on *Forbes'* list of highest female earners.[6] Ill-wishers may whisper that Lady Gaga is past her prime, but that remains to be seen. She still shows sufficient inspiration and is able to present herself as one big living work of art. In the song 'Applause,' she refers to pop art – turns the tables on it, in fact: '*One second I'm a Koons, then suddenly the Koons is me / Pop culture was in art, now art's in pop culture in me.*' Her music, provocative video clips, highly in-dividual dress sense, ever-changing hairdos and tattoos have indeed brought her a long way. Her audience is important to her. Little wonder then that she refers to them as her 'little monsters' and that she (allegedly) writes her Tweets herself, sharing her vicissitudes with them. This results in an authen-tic image of an exceptional person and gives the audience a feeling of being close to their idol.

Where is the middleman?

Of course, whether tens of millions of little monsters can all really be close to their idol at the same time is another matter. *The Financial Times* paradoxically referred to this phenomenon as 'mass intimacy'. In any case there is no traditional middleman mediating: Lady Gaga communicates to her fans directly. This communication is both quick and direct, and the fans' enthusiasm translates not only into sales figures, but also into a feeling of solidarity.

Lady Gaga didn't come up with this all by herself, of course. She has a big team behind her in Los Angeles, talent managers and communications staff led by Troy Carter, a modern-day record executive with one of his offices in Palo Alto, in the heart of America's high-tech hub Silicon Val-ley. Here, they are not concerned so much with PR as with state-of-the-art technology. Since 2011, Carter and his people have been working on a new social media platform called Backplane, which brings together all content and interaction for a particular star in one place. The idea behind Backplane was to drastically change the economics of Hollywood, with the artist at the centre rather than the record company.[7] This meshed perfectly with Lady Gaga's approach: she was already actively involved in discussions on her many fan sites, which means she not only exudes authenticity, but also embodies it through her actions.

Backplane illustrates something else as well. Ever since its launch, the company has been losing money hand over fist, in spite of the millions pumped into it.[8] What gives? Lady Gaga's website https://littlemonsters.com was able to bring a million fans together, making it a huge success as a dedicated social media platform, but the same logic didn't transfer to other brands. It quickly transpired that few people wanted a new, brand-specific platform alongside Facebook and Instagram. So by no means all new platforms succeed just on the basis of their form. Copying or slightly modifying a tried-and-tested concept is no guarantee of success. Backplane has now replaced its CEO and is embarking on a new strategy, as many start-ups in Silicon Valley have to on a regular basis.

The entertainment industry is not an island: changes are taking place in many different sectors, often driven by technological developments that are seeing traditional mediating roles disappear to be replaced by new platforms. To linger at the music industry for some moments, I give two clear-cut examples: Spotify and Apple's iTunes Store.

The new player: Spotify

A Swedish start-up, Spotify was launched in 2008. The company started from nothing but in 2014 had more than 40 million active users, 10 million paying customers, was turning over more than 1 billion dollars and was worth an estimated 10 billion-plus dollars.[9] Spotify is the fresh new rival to at least four existing sources of music: illegal downloads, radio, CDs and online sales through the iTunes Store.

Spotify has paid subscriptions, but a free version is still available as well. In terms of cost, it still resembles illegal downloading (it is free); in terms of approach, it is more like radio (turn it on and Spotify will find more good songs for you); and in terms of freedom of choice, it resembles CDs and online sales (it is easy to find most things you want).

This has led to a number of interesting developments. Firstly, it is a combination of the cheap (listening to the radio) and the expensive (buying CDs). Secondly, everyone is now a DJ, blurring the distinction between listener and provider. Thirdly, it has lowered the threshold for publishing music. Together, these developments mean that traditional radio stations, music stores and other intermediaries are under more pressure than they already were before Spotify arrived on the scene.

So a merging of roles is taking place and the hierarchy is being disrupted. Where a reasonably rigid order used to exist, we now make connections ever more easily – and just as easily break them. This is opening up endless possibilities, but also creating great uncertainty. Later in this book, I will attempt to represent these changes in a model, which I call the 'diopticon': a reality in which everyone can enter into interactions with everyone else.

The Very Hungry Caterpillar: Apple

Let's focus now on another star in the modern business firmament: Apple, a company which, unlike newcomer Spotify, did have something to lose when it started getting involved with music. Apple had been teetering on the brink of the abyss and only just started achieving some success again under founder Steve Jobs, who had been away for a while. In 2001, the company had a turnover of 8 billion dollars – not exactly small change. The next year, Jobs introduced the iPod, a music player that proved popular with gadget lovers. The little wheel on the iPod seemed to be Apple's biggest new innovation. But it only seemed to be: when the company stopped producing the original version of the iPod in 2014, the real innovation in retrospect turned out to lie somewhere else entirely.

The biggest innovation of all was the metamorphosis of Apple from computer manufacturer into supplier of a complete package. This package consists of content (music, films, apps), the equipment all this runs smoothly on, the hipness of a strong brand, and finally the provision of access to the rest of the world through the web, telephony, text messages, WhatsApp, Facebook, et cetera. Apple is a Very Hungry Caterpillar: the company is market leader in total solutions for the digital end user, but is still looking for new opportunities for growth.

The contrast between the current generation of Apple gadgets and Apple's first computer is enormous. Apple was a wooden box you had to assemble yourself and which wasn't useful for anything until you, the user, thought up and programmed an interesting application for it. Apple now has an application for everything: from telephony to keeping an eye on your weight. And you can't open the box anymore; if you try it, you'll void your warranty.

All these changes have been extremely fruitful for Apple: in 2015, the company booked a turnover of 234 billion dollars.

Five points and a warning

So far we have discussed:
- Society and the economy are changing at an incredible pace, driven by the ongoing march of technological development
- This is bringing the huge players (the Pope, Lady Gaga, Apple) into contact with the little people (you and me)

in a completely new way, with all the risks this brings for
them and for your privacy and freedom of choice

- As a result, existing organisations have to constantly reinvent themselves to survive
- For the middle, all this is resulting both in pain and interesting new opportunities
- Dynamic, sleek, flexible platforms are emerging.

As a warning to big companies, I would like to present the
example of Eastman Kodak. In its heyday, the photographic
company employed 145,000 people. It invented the digital
camera, but put plans to develop this further on ice. In the
year Kodak filed for bankruptcy (2012), the photo sharing
website Instagram was sold by Facebook for in excess of 1 billion dollars. At the time, Instagram employed just 15 people
and Facebook only 5,000.[10]

The motto is: implement change in time. When you are
fighting for your life, it is often too late. Not all companies
are flexible enough to be able to make fundamental changes
to their business model in time. Korean electronics giant
Samsung started out selling noodles. For Samsung, the way
ahead was clear.

From giant to bear

Above, I discussed giants and said something about the
middlemen who have been swept away and replaced by reinvented intermediaries. In the case of the Pope, this meant
new faces in the retirement home that until recently was the
Catholic Church; in the case of Lady Gaga, it was an agent
who is taking the wind out of the sails of the record company
executives by making connections between PR and technology.

Things are changing – not only at the top and middle segments of the hierarchical ladder, but also at the bottom. Individuals, believers and fans are more demanding. They have become prosumers of their idols, like Facebook users who are not principally customers, but co-creators of their own brands.

Technology is always a leitmotif in this development: it develops rapidly, and the opportunities it brings are determining the revolutionary changes society and the economy are currently undergoing.

For insight into revolutions, we travel to Russia: a country that spent seventy years in thrall to another revolution – that of Marx and Lenin. Two gentlemen who quite rightly wanted to divide the pie more fairly, but who underestimated the impact of other revolutions – including the rise of the information society and the opportunities this offers to workers.

In the age of Marx and Lenin, relations within society were rigid: divided vertically into classes and horizontally into occupations. In practice, their model was set in stone, again with a clear horizontal and vertical organisational structure: the successful capitalist formula, but distributed more fairly. This turned out to be a rather bad idea.

Now, the stone structure of our society is starting to lose its solidity. In fact, it is starting to crumble. It takes extreme conditions to do this and there are many such extreme conditions in Siberia, where we are heading next.

From fixed to fluid

A few years ago, I travelled to Novosibirsk, where it was actually pretty warm. The weather in this Siberian city is a climatological roller coaster, with an average mid-day temperature of –12 °C in January and +25 °C in July. When I visited the city, it was almost 30 °C. There's not much to do there, since Novosibirsk is mainly about heavy industry, including mechanical engineering, smelting, electrical engineering and the arms industry. The place I found worthiest of a visit was Novosibirskij Akademgorodok ('Novosibirsk Academic Town'), founded in 1957 on the banks of a reservoir as a campus for privileged academics. Both the lake and the town were built by engineers during the Khrushchev era, when Stalinism was being renounced. Most of the statues of the Man of Steel were taken down and people in the Soviet Union could breathe a little more easily. In the academic world, this led to the creation of little islands where brilliant minds could occupy themselves with scientific innovation in relative freedom. Akademgorodok was such an island.

In the years following the demise of the Soviet Union, Akademgorodok suffered greatly: the institutes had to close and most of the academics lost their living. But now the place is back on the map. Giants such as IBM, Intel and Schlumberger have brought work and investment. The government is also contributing considerable investment: during the period from 2012 to 2017 approximately 10 billion Roubles (150 million Euros).[11] Research is being carried out at 35 research institutes. This research town is being referred to as Silicon Forest, in reference to the Karakan Pine Forest on the banks of the reservoir.[12]

Three transitions

In Siberia, it's natural to think about phase transitions. Due to extreme temperatures in winter, boiling water freezes in just a few seconds when thrown off a balcony, as a funny Youtube video demonstrates. Also, the aftereffects of the demise of the Soviet Union show how a society can rise and then fall again with changing conditions. I'll now switch to current reality and present three trends I believe are changing our society in such a way that we can say it has become fluid.

The first of these is transparency as a global megatrend. The Pope and Lady Gaga are Twittering away like mad – but it doesn't stop there. Worldwide, people are giving insights into their everyday lives *and* into the world around them through Tweets, videos or blogs. Governments are seeing how their information is being made public, and are using big data to steer their policies; companies not only have more data at their fingertips, but are having to justify their activities. The consequences of and possibilities opened up by such transparency are so endless I refer to this as 'radical transparency'.

The second trend is that individuals and organisations are getting more and more opportunities to carry out small-scale activities that used to be the exclusive preserve of big players: everyone is now his or her own travel agent, energy supplier, hotelier, publisher and activist. Consumers have become prosumers. Government power is taken less for granted, and large companies are being forced to ask them-selves searching questions about the roles they want to play in the future, and what the consequences of these will be. The scale at which change is taking place is so enormous that I refer to this as 'radical decentralisation'.

The third of these trends is the end of the middle. In the same way liquids do not have a middle, organisations and society as a whole also no longer have a middle – at least, not in the organised way we are accustomed to. I am talking about a middle in two different senses here: a role (interme-diary or middleman) and on a scale (a relative position).

I will now elaborate briefly on these three trends, before discussing them in greater detail over the course of the book. One consequence of these three trends is that we have to find tailor-made solutions to our various problems. This is leading to big changes for individuals, companies and governments.

Radical transparency

Transparency has become something of a magic word: an aim in itself (for government bodies); a means (for the improvement of processes) and an inescapable reality (Edward Snowden is a living example).

A good (but horrible) illustration of the latter – transparency is here to stay – is a case involving British Petroleum. When the Deepwater Horizon drilling platform exploded in 2010, causing a massive oil slick, it was possible to follow the situation 24 hours a day from a webcam. You could easily stick the window in the corner of your monitor. BP tried to limit the damage to its public image, but this proved impossible: internet users were able to see with their own eyes what was going on. Press reports put out by BP trying to sway public opinion had less effect than a public discussion based on facts and observations available to everyone.

In other words, the discussion about BP was transparent, in the same way that the editing history of an article on Wikipedia is transparent. It is no longer possible to hush things up or secretly take sides. Governments are now also feeling this, thanks to that other 'wiki' application: Wikileaks. Secret messages from the American diplomatic service, the escapades of Mr and Mrs Assad of Syria: suddenly, it is all online. Institutions can choose to react by making a conscious choice to make sensitive information public: it saves spending a whole load of money on security. In Norway, tax returns are public by law, so it was a small step to make all this data accessible on the internet. Now, everyone can check whether the neighbours' nice new SUV was purchased with money he earned legitimately or not.

It's not only government that is becoming more transparent: citizens are too. This is not a problem when they share their adventures on Twitter or Facebook (and doens't regret it later). Facebook, however, collects a lot more data than that. Max Schrems, a law student in Austria, asked the company for an overview of all the information it had on him. To his surprise, his request was granted. He got a stack of paper he could hardly carry. Facebook is acting like a private detective on a massive scale, selling the information it obtains to the highest bidder.

There is another rather creepy example from the world of entertainment. Disney World has a go-ahead attitude to transparency. The company has set up a new website under the name My Disney Experience, linked to an app on mobile phones. You can use this app to book time slots for attractions and in Disney's restaurants. The app has a few built-in functionalities that mean Disney gets all the information it wants on its visitors. The names and personal details of visitors are passed on to the staff in the theme park so they can entertain you even better. A little girl might ask: 'How does Snow White know my name, mummy?'[13] Of course, the exact reason is a little too complex to explain, but you could simply say: 'Because everyone knows everything about you, darling.'

Radical decentralisation

My grandmother listened to the priest every week for moral guidance and read the right newspaper to keep up with the news. The benevolent State made sure the biggest social problems were solved. People worked hard, but most of the time lived on automatic pilot. We can no longer do this. The advance of technology means that, although all sorts of things are being automated, our lives are less automatic than they used to be.

The current state of information and communications technology is making new forms of communication possible, offering us access to a huge amount of up-to-date information, and thus are changing the role we play as citizens. This is the time of 'power to the people'. Not as a hollow slogan, but rather a concrete development allowing citizens to get on with implementing their own solutions. In 2010, *The Economist* portrayed the new British Prime Minister David Cameron with a mohican in the colours of the Union Jack. His radical activism: contracting out government tasks to small groups of citizens.

Fortunately, life throws up all manner of opportunities for free citizens to set their own course, facilitated by technology. In fact, we have to set our own course now: the priest has lost his power and the State no longer provides the guidance it used to.

Radical decentralisation is everywhere. More and more matters can be better organised by the individual, or at least on a small rather than large scale. It used to be that a big coal-fired power station was needed to provide everyone with energy – now all you need is a solar panel or a wind turbine. Smart groups of citizens are making this economically feasible, and other groups are able to purchase the energy generated at a low price. The successful power companies of the future will act more like brokers than suppliers. The same goes for the hotel sector: previously, travel agencies would book rooms in bulk from big hotel chains, but now a handy website provides direct contact between supply and demand. Airbnb means everyone can be a hotelier and a customer at the same time.

With a good idea, a network and a strategy, anyone can have a big impact on society – faster than ever before. This implies that we have to combine commercial and social interests to create a new form of public commerce. Technology is playing a facilitating role in the creation, maintenance and application of a network, both literally and figuratively. This will not happen without resistance, however, as the institutions that represent the power of the old economy are trying to restrict the power of individuals and small organisations. Nevertheless, there will come a moment when they will be forced to make way for new, creative ideas – but it could be a while before radical decentralisation has taken root everywhere.

The squeeze on the middle

This fluid reality no longer has a middle as we know it. When I say middle, I mean both the roles in the middle and the middle of a scale.

By roles in the middle, I mean the middlemen, go-betweens or intermediaries. A middleman could be out of work because people are finding everything, making everything and doing everything themslves; examples include travel agents, hoteliers, publishers and charities. A lot of other intermediaries who are still in work, such as bankers and employment agencies, are having to radically rethink their strategies and working practices. For others, new opportunities are arising, such as the educational technologist who forms a link between education and technology.

Then there is the scale. People and organisations that are in the middle in terms of size or income are in difficulty, e.g. the traditional middle-class. Their jobs are under particular pressure. Some small and medium-sized enterprises are also experiencing problems: too big to act as a flexible core organisation, but too small to organise the required talent and knowledge in a dynamic, efficient way.

The middle has always been susceptible to squeezing. This applies to middle managers, and not only those of the human race. In an interesting research project, academics from universities in Manchester and Liverpool set out to analyse stress among managers. Their conclusion was that middle managers are subject to greater stresses than either their bosses or their subordinates. They reached this conclusion by studying apes at Chester Zoo, looking for expressions of dominance and submission. It turned out the apes in the middle of the hierarchy had the highest levels of stress hormones. The reason for this, it was said, was that these apes have most conflicts: with the apes above them *and* with the apes below them. According to the researchers, the same applies to human middle managers.

Under all this strain, the middle is fighting back tooth and nail, and will not disappear overnight. Lady Gaga has not cut out the middleman entirely, as she continues to work with traditional, mainstream labels. Streamline and Interscope, big market players, released her 2013 album *artpop*. However Bruce Houghton, music expert at hypebot,com, stated with some satisfaction: 'It is a sign of real progress that their tactics no longer work anything like as well as they did.' The poor middle – always a difficult position, but because of the advance of technology, radical transparency and decentralisation the only remaining option is change.

Fluid change

I have sketched three developments that represent a society in flux: radical transparency, radical decentralisation and a radically different middle. That is, if any middle remains at all, as it hardly makes sense to envisage a 'middle' when talking about a transition from solid to liquid.

I am not the first to use the word 'liquid' as a metaphor for social change. That was Zygmunt Bauman, a Polish-British sociologist and philosopher of Jewish descent who (partly on the grounds of his ethnicity) fled Communist Poland and broke through in the West with his thinking about modernity. I quote a passage from the beginning of his wide-ranging book *Liquid Modernity* (2000):

> *'To 'be modern' means to modernize – compulsively, obsessively; not so much just 'to be,' let alone to keep its identity intact, but forever 'becoming,' avoiding completion, staying underdefined. Each new structure which replaces the previous one as soon as it is declared old-fashioned and past its use-by date is only another momentary settlement – acknowledged as temporary and 'until further notice.' What was some time ago dubbed (erroneously)Top of Form 'post-modernity,' and what I've chosen to call, more to the point, 'liquid modernity,' is the growing conviction that change is the only permanence, and uncertainty the only certainty. A hundred years ago 'to be modern' meant to chase 'the final state of perfection' – now it means an infinity of improvement, with no 'final state' in sight and none desired.*[14]

He therefore sets himself apart from the post-modernists, who see a radical break with the past. Instead, he sees fluidity as part of modernity in its current form. Unlike Bauman, I believe that we are experiencing a rather abrupt break with the past, that forces humanity to define its modernity in a new way. In less than half a generation – roughly between 1995 and 2010 – everyone has got access to a computer, a mobile telephone and social media. Business use and personal use have merged and countless inventions have been given applications other than those for which they were created. The acceleration of the pace of change this has brought about has given rise to a new form of modernity characterised principally – and here I concur with Bauman – by permanent technological development and social change.

In summary

The journey has only just begun. I started this chapter in a centuries-old, megalomaniacal institution: the Vatican. I ended it with Zygmunt Bauman in a liquid era.

I will now continue my exploration of how the individual relates to the giants and what this means for the middle. But first, in Chapter 2 I will talk about innovation. I will start with the exponential growth of technology, proceed to talk about robots and end with capitalism. In Chapter 3, I will look at a number of giant technology companies, big data and its discontents. Then, in Chapter 4, I will describe the liquefied middle on the basis of a model I call the 'diopticon'. Personal change will be dealt with in Chapter 5, and in Chapter 6 I will devote attention to employment and the middle class. Chapter 7 examines power, using the metaphor of a melting diamond. The final chapter is then dedicated to the search for your own talent (and that of others).

2

Gigantic innovation
On technological development, robots and disruptive progress

In the previous chapter, I discussed several key terms: radical transparency, radical decentralisation and the liquid society. The very big and very small are coming together and the middle is disappearing or has to reinvent itself. In spite of decentralisation, the 'biggest' are not dying out completely. In this chapter, I will describe a number of contemporary giants: players and developments on the grandest scale, which on the one hand are making developments possible but on the other sometimes act as a brake. I will start with technological development. The question is no longer if robots (and other forms of automation) will do more, but when.

Pisces a natura determinati sunt ad natandum, magni at minores
comedendum
(Fish are destined by nature to swim; the big to eat the small.')
Baruch Spinoza[15]

Big Blue

In the 1960s and '70s, IBM and components manufacturer Intel were the first big players in the field of modern electronics. Both companies still exist. IBM is affectionately known as 'Big Blue' and, with an annual research budget of 6 billion dollars, it certainly is rather big. IBM holds the world record for requesting patents (although Microsoft and Oracle spend more on this), which speaks volumes about IBM's role as an innovator. The company made its name with first-generation computers: huge, punch-card devouring beasts.

The fact that IBM still exists at such a scale is really something of a miracle. The company's top managers politely refused (more than once) when Bill Gates tried to sell his company Microsoft to them – and this is not the only example of their less than perspicacious vision of the future. 'I think there is a world market for maybe five computers,' a top IBM manager is supposed to have said in 1943, although the provenance of this quote is disputed. The latter also applies to a comment attributed to Bill Gates, the driving force behind the personal computer, which began to flourish following the invention of the microchip, making computers available to individuals. He is supposed to have said that 640 kilobytes would be enough memory for every application on a computer: '*It's enough for everybody*'. A ridiculous statement in hindsight; these days, even the chip on a bank card has more capacity.

The point is that people – including people with considerable knowledge of the subject and careers in Silicon Valley – continue to underestimate the speed at which technology is developing. I deliberately say 'is developing' and not 'is being developed' here, because technological development seems to have become an autonomous entity. The speed of development is now such a natural law that the people putting it in motion themselves seem to be playing supporting roles. The play has taken on a life of its own and the actors have become the audience.

Such a 'natural law' was observed fifty years ago by Gordon Moore. It means, roughly speaking, that every year computers are doubling their computing capacity for the same price. Doubling every year – that's pretty rapid growth. So rapid, most people don't realise what this really means in practice. You can work out whether you are one of these people by doing a simple test.

Take a sheet of A4 paper. Fold it, then fold the folded sheet again and so on until you have folded the sheet of paper ten times. Ask yourself before you start whether you think it will be possible. Most people think it will be – folding a piece of paper ten times is child's play, right? So now give it a go.

And? It didn't work, did it? A piece of paper folded ten times would be thicker than two packs of standard paper – about ten centimetres thick – and no one can fold that. If you were to carry on folding another ten times, the sheet of paper would be more than 10 kilometres thick – quite a feat for a sheet of paper.

Another good example involves saving money. Imagine you find an old post office savings bank book in your family archives. A hundred years ago, your great-grandfather deposited 10 dollars, pounds or marks in the account (a considerable amount of money in those days!). You go to the bank that took over the post office savings bank to cash in the account. How much would you get? Quite likely nothing, because the bank may have canceled old bank books ages ago. If the bank actually felt generous and decided to pay out, your fortune would depend on the rate of interest. If the interest rate was 1 percent per annum, you would get € 12.27. If the interest over that period was 2 percent a year, you'd go home with € 32.87. If the interest rate was 10 percent, you'd get a tidy € 62,533.69.

Moore and technology

Exponential growth is a feature of many other aspects of computer technlogy, such as storage capacity (on a hard drive or other medium), the number of pixels on the screen, and the transfer speed of data over a network.

There is evidence that Moore's law can be applied very broadly, and not only to computer technology. In fact, research by the Sante Fe Institute and MIT has shown it to be applicable to 62 different technologies.[16, 17] Two examples are wind energy technology and the technology used to decipher DNA; in both cases, the costs per unit are decreasing at the same rate.

The same applies to the speed at which the number of users of Facebook or Twitter has grown during recent years: such specific applications have been experiencing exponential growth for some time now. Every now and then, a paradigm shift has to take place; growth that brings the adoption to an innovation within reach. One day, suitable successors to Facebook and Twitter will come along. What exactly these will be like, we can't yet tell. However, the fact that something new will come along is indisputable. In other words: technology tends to develop in stages. If you add all the developments together, you will see that this exponential trend is ongoing.

The basis of this continuous growth is the ever-decreasing cost of technology that at present is out of reach, while smart techies are already coming up with applications now that can be made into a prototype in two years' time and in four years' time will be within reach of the masses.

Hundreds of start-ups are using this method, backed up by business cases, to induce financiers to invest in technology in development. For example, there are countless ideas and initiatives to make our lives easier (or more difficult) using big data. These all need storage capacity and processing power, both of which are constantly getting cheaper, thanks to exponential growth. In practice, we see that this data is in fact accumulating at the ever cheaper storage available in server farms. Figure 2.1 shows the amount of digital data in the world. The makers of this graph have also had a go at predicting the future on the basis of ongoing exponential growth. I will look at big data in greater depth in Chapter 3.

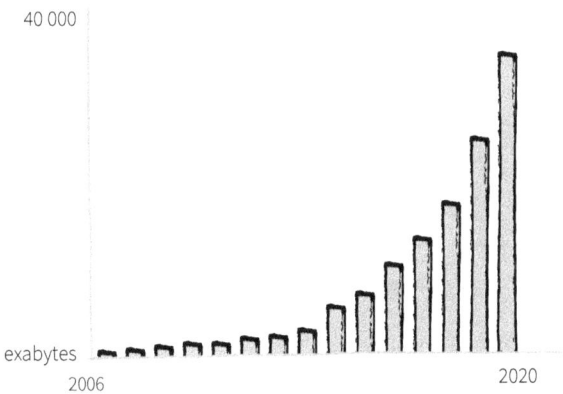

Figure 2.1

Moore and man

Technology developing at a rapid pace is one thing, but what about mankind? Surely human beings are not changing as fast as technology – or so many people think. The following argument was defended in *The Financial Times*: '*It appears that – for all the level of technology change and interest in the power of engineering to create radical shifts in how the world works – the ability of humans to make sense of it all may not be increasing at the same rate as innovation activity over-all*'.[18]

I have my doubts about this uncertainty concerning the speed at which people can keep pace with technological change. This can be seen in the growth of the two well-known websites Airbnb and Facebook (Figure 2.2). In the case of Airbnb, this is reflected by the numbers of guests, and in the case of Facebook by the numbers of active users worldwide. Here too, we see extremely strong growth, which looks very similar to exponential growth.

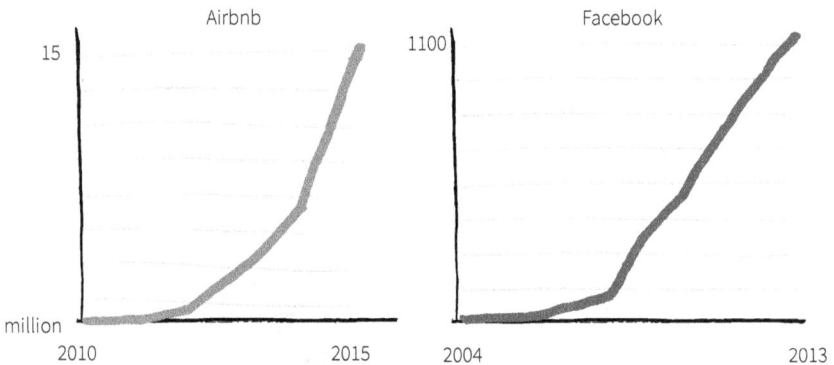

Figure 2.2

So where is all this leading?

Nevertheless, a note of warning to anyone who might be tempted to think that the sky's the limit: it isn't. To keep things a bit more down to earth, let's look at the development of the global population. Figure 2.3 shows how the world's population has developed from the beginnings of humanity until now.

Estimated world population

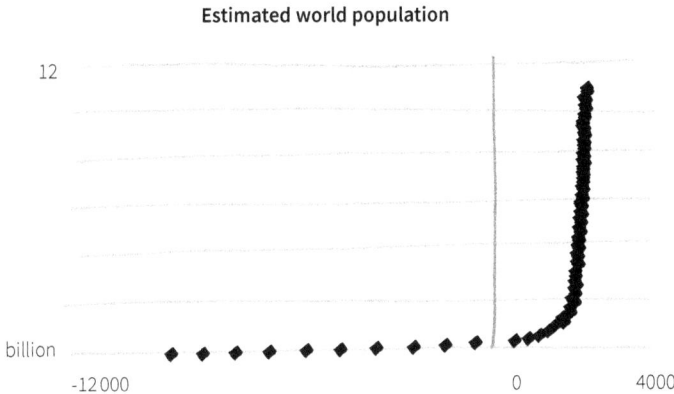

Figure 2.3

The speed of this growth is breath-taking. Could we be looking at exponential growth here? Let's look at the same data, but zooming in on a specific period. Figure 2.4 shows global population development in the past fifty or so years and from roughly 1900 to 2100 – estimates have been made in relation to both the past and the future.

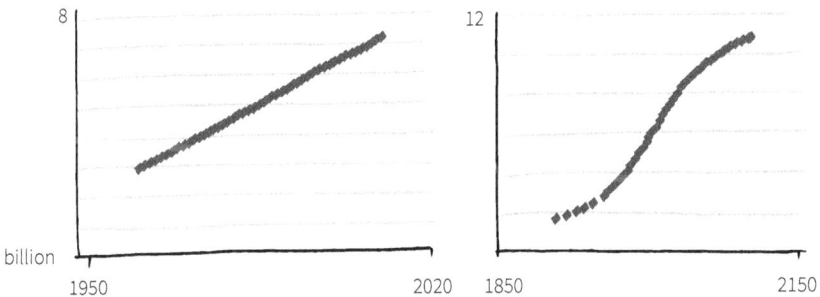

Figure 2.4

It is clear that, in both periods, the population of the world is not growing exponentially. During the past fifty years growth has levelled off, with the same amount of people being added in each time unit. In the period 1900-2100, the curve shot up again, before levelling off again later. Maximum growth will have been reached around the year 2200.[19]

Which is a good thing: there is only so much space on earth, so population growth will have to end some time.

The end of Moore

As with population growth, the speed of technological growth will also have to level off at some point. If Moore's law continues, in five hundred years' time a computer will have more bits than there are particles in the universe, which would probably be a little excessive. But when will the critical point be reached?

According to IBM researchers, we are fast approaching the limit of placing transistors on a chip. If the distance in the chips is smaller than 7 nanometres, the computer becomes unreliable. We are currently at 22 nanometres. IBM is trying to keep the rapid advance going for the time being by using nanotubes.

This does not mean, however, that this growth will stop. Futurologist Ray Kurzweil, entrepreneur and author of interesting books on technology and the future, has put forward the paradigm shift as a solution. At a certain point, progress leads to a completely new form of progress. To illustrate this, Kurzweil effortlessly compares the evolution of intelligent man, the transition from the stone age to the bronze and iron ages, the introduction of television and the invention of the internet.[20] Such paradigm shifts, Kurzweil argues, are taking place with increasing frequency. He sketches a future made up of machines that are far more intelligent than people and extra-terrestrial colonies where technology continues to develop. In the meantime, he is swallowing enough vitamin pills in order to experience it all personally.

If one technology leads to the development of the next, in time we will ake the transition. For example, we now know for sure that we will switch from the hard drive with moving parts to data storage on chips; this transition is well under way now that ssds (solid state drives) have become reasonably affordable in the laptops segment. We also know that there will come a day when the current fourth-generation mobile network no longer fulfils requirements. Some things we do not know, however: what leaps in use the next generation of devices will make possible, and what technological leap will be required to then supersede these applications. Something will make the computer as we know it now redundant – what that is, we don't yet know. And once this new 'thing' has arrived, it will in turn disrupt our social reality in a way we can't yet foresee. The development of devices and applications is as unpredictable and stage-driven as the development of technology is gradual and predictable in general terms.

All this plays into the hands of science fiction authors and the wealthy institutes that are busy inventing our new futures in their laboratories. In 2011, the company D-Wave Systems came up with a quantum computer, a computer that has done away with the zeros and ones of transistors and makes use instead of the superpositions of particles, from zero to one and everything in between. This results in exponentially greater storage and faster data processing. The first prototypes are currently under construction. In twenty years, maybe we will all have a mini quantum computer implanted under our skin, making our lives easier. How? I'll leave that up to your imagination.

Blinkered to past and future

Do we really need continuous technological development? This question doesn't really seem very relevant. After all, those who have predicted the future on the basis of existing needs have always been proved wrong. In 1977, Ken Oslon (founder of DEC, the Digital Equipment Corporation) said: 'There is no reason anyone would want a computer in their home.' This turned out to be a massive miscalculation.

This comment – and there are many other examples – shows that even people involved with technological innovation at a professional level can be mistaken when looking ahead. So what chance does the 'man in the street' have of peering into the future? The inability and unwillingness of citizens and politicians to take the steps needed to put an end to the overexploitation of the earth illustrates this. 'Steady as she goes' seems to be the consensus position.

The same applies the other way around: we find it difficult to imagine the past and draw lessons from it. I personally have trouble imagining the pre-digital era – in spite of the fact I was actually there. I imagine medieval peasants, huddled shivering on a few sheepskins in a damp hut. I'm exaggerating, of course, but it is true that we become accustomed to advances in technology so quickly that everything that came before suddenly seems prehistoric. The world wide web and other advances which – as you will often hear – 'are now an integral part of society' fit me like a favourite old winter coat. We are blinkered to both the past and the future, and live as if time stands still.

So how fast has all this happened? The very first digital computer was built in 1946. At that time, we'd had railways for over a hundred years, air-conditioning for half a century and (unfortunately) atomic bombs for a year. Internet is a more recent development. In 2014, we celebrated an anniversary in Pakhuis De Zwijger in Amsterdam: 25 years of in-

ternet in the Netherlands – the second country in the world
to go online, in 1988. (I can say with some pride that we were
trendsetters.) I got my first e-mail account in 1994, with De
Digitale Stad (DDS). I don't remember how hard I had to
push my parents for this, but I do remember how exciting it
was exploring the virtual city through the brand new digital
superhighway.

There is a fantastic video clip from 1994 of a conversation
between one of the driving forces behind DDS and parlia-
mentary spokesman Nicolas Cramer; they are discussing
easy access to information. Cramer thinks that 'making
everything available just like that, at the press of a button,
could lead to the opposite effect. That you actually make the
gap even bigger; that people have even more of a feeling of,
what on earth am I actually doing?' It's strange looking back
on that movie now. I can't imagine what I'd do without Google or e-mail.

Moore's law describes a 'steady drumbeat' that is not
going to stop any time soon. And it's relevant not only to the
development of computer chips, but also other computer
components, very different technologies and – last but not
least – the use of technology by flesh-and-blood human beings. This growth often occurs in stages, with one technology
being superseded by another when the first has reached the
limits of its growth. Where this growth will end, we don't yet
know.

The robots are coming

I must admit I shed a tear or two when watching the animated film *Wall-E* (2008). In this poignant story about human
hope, two robots come together and outdo man in terms of
humanity, but not before a good dose of cultural pessimism
has come along.

Whether robots will actually turn out to be so benign naturally remains to be seen. There are many films in which things go dramatically wrong because robots no longer serve humanity, but rather oppress or even eradicate man. A good example of this is *I, Robot*, a box-office hit from 2004 starring Will Smith. The film starts with the three laws of robotics intended to protect humanity – which are subsequently broken. These laws are:

- *Law 1: A robot may not injure a human being or, through inaction, allow a human being to come to harm.*
- *Law 2: A robot must obey the orders given it by human beings except where such orders would conflict with the First Law.*
- *Law 3: A robot must protect its own existence as long as such protection does not conflict with the First or Second Laws.*

The filmmakers didn't pluck these laws out of thin air: they are taken from prescient science fiction author Isaac Asimov, who introduced them in his 1942 short story 'Runaround.'[21] The collection in which this story is included is also called *I, Robot* and is certainly worth a read.

My definition of robot is a loose one: a machine designed to help us – a cybernetic slave, in effect. I would add that it has to be able to communicate with us. I consider the robot's limbs – the actuation a lot of people in robotics are working on – to be less important. I find their relationship to man and man's needs more important than physical characteristics.

Four robots

To illustrate the importance of robots in human society, I use a graph with two axes – see Figure 2.5. The horizontal axis shows the degree of autonomy or independence of robots.

Some robots work to a clear step-by-step plan, or have to be given an instruction before doing anything; other robots can work out and perform their next task by themselves, and can even deal with changing circumstances. The vertical axis shows the degree of complexity of the robot brain: the level of complexity of the calculations performed and the scope of the data involved. I have given the four types different names.

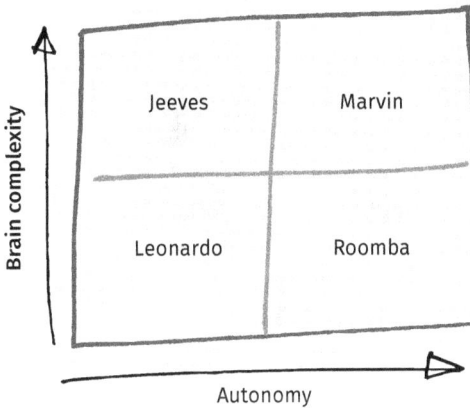

Figure 2.5

Leonardo

At bottom left – not autonomous and not very complex – is the type of robot I call Leonardo, a piece of equipment controlled directly by a human.

The historical Leonardo da Vinci, Renaissance inventor, scientist and artist, not only had a very high level of all-round development, but could also think extremely quickly and was extremely versatile. However, I named this type of robot after the Da Vinci robot from Intuitive Surgical, Inc., a machine that helps perform complex operations in the operating room. This robot consists of two parts. The first is a device with four arms that can pass through small openings in the patient. These arms and their tentacles have much greater freedom of movement and precision than the human hand and wrist. The human doctor stands at a control panel, which is the second piece of this robot. The surgeon sees enlarged, three-dimensional images and operates the robot arms using handles.

Da Vinci is an extremely useful innovation for hospitals because of the machine's physical properties, which exceed those of a person in a few very specific ways. It also offers additional potential in terms of remote working, recording procedures and cooperation. Nevertheless, this robot is just a tool: only as good and as useful as the surgeon using it. In fact, it is (almost literally) an extension of the surgeon.

Other robots in the Leonardo category include the robots that help build cars and screw the tops onto tubes of toothpaste in factories. They are fast, accurate and don't complain – ideal employees for work that demands no initiative.

Many computer programmes can also be seen as Leonardos. Word processors, for example: very handy as a typewriter-plus, which can also help perform repetitive actions such as layout and macros.

Finally, there are the 3D printers that can print out all kinds of things: from aircraft parts to guns. You can now buy a simple one for just a few hundred Euros. Just feed the printer the material it needs and it will make you … nothing at all. To work, it needs a programme that tells the printer exactly how to print the object you want.

Roomba

Do you have one of those cool Roomba robot vacuum cleaners? These little revolving domestic slaves are all the rage. Roomba is a dish-shaped machine that finds its own way through your home, sucking up the dust as it goes. It can work away happily all day long without you lifting a finger. Millions of these devices have been sold, and it's not just their human owners who are thrilled with them: cats love them too, as they can jump on board and be carried around or massaged by the unpredictable movements.

Roomba is autonomous, moves around your living room by itself, but is really very stupid. It probably comes as no surprise that your five-year-old daughter can probably vacuum more efficiently than Roomba.

Comparable to Roomba, albeit in a very different context, is the 'personal assistant' that tries to help you with the word processor referred to above. You may well be able to relate to my frustration when Microsoft Word starts to think for itself, usually costing me more time than it saves. I generally snuff out such demonstrations of initiative before they can do too much damage.

Eliza deserves an honourable mention in the Roomba category. Eliza is a pioneering computer programme, developed in the 1960s and still widely available online, acting as a psychiatrist. You say something to Eliza and she will say something back, often in the form of a follow-up question. But even if you fall for it fairly easily on the first go, the programme is actually deceptively simple. If you keep the questions coming, Eliza soon gets out of her depth.

Finally, I would like to refer to the countless characters that populate the incomparable computer game *Grand Theft Auto v*. This is an 'open world game' in which you can move around freely (and shoot people or run them over). Many other creatures roam around freely at the same time, but they exist only in the computer's brain. Trying following one of these characters through the streets of the fictional city of Los Santos some time – I'd be willing to bet your life is considerably more interesting than his.

Jeeves

At top left in the diagram you will find Jeeves – a robot that is not autonomous (he waits for your questions), but does have a lot of computing power. I named him after the (now retired) virtual butler who used to serve ask.com, a search engine that never got past Google. I could just as easily have called him Google.

Jeeves was an innovation in the world of search engines because of the possibility to ask questions in natural language, instead of having to enter search terms. This addition soon proved to be rather insignificant, a little novelty that users quickly lost interest in. The reason for this is that it gave the appearance of autonomy that the computer didn't really have.

Other examples include the immense databases we now use for all kinds of purposes: Wikipedia as an encyclopaedia, Google as our guide through the gigantic repository of text, images and sounds, but also the programmes behind big data used by security services to spy on you.

None of these 'robots' can be said to be independent. Sales site Amazon, for example, makes suggestions of books you might like on the basis of what other people have found interesting. Which is very useful, but to date Amazon itself has never read a book – let alone written one.

Marvin

In the fourth quadrant is Marvin, named after Marvin the Paranoid Android, the hilarious brainchild of Douglas Adams and a character in his *The Hitchhiker's Guide to the Galaxy* novels (and the film based on them). He has been functioning completely autonomously for billions of years and is highly intelligent (and, as a side-effect, rather depressed).

Marvin is a great caricature, and with 50,000 times the intelligence of a human being a superlative degree of man's bad traits, perhaps a precursor of the robots of the future. Other robots from the science fiction genre have adopted other bad human characteristics, such as the urge to dominate – examples from popular culture include *The Terminator*, *R.U.R.* and *I, Robot*.

In the meantime, we humans are busily creating Marvins to autonomously perform tasks based on their ability to process gigantic quantities of data at an equally impressive speed.

This has led to Watson, a gigantic supercomputer project by IBM. The first assignment given to this supercomputer was to play the long-running quiz *Jeopardy*, in which the players have to come up with the right question on the basis of a clue. Watson won the quiz in 2011, and IBM is now conquering the business market with Watson – the company recently invested a billion dollars in doing just that. The result was just 100 million in turnover in the first three years,[22] but it is a promising development: the capacity to reason and to deal with natural language makes it a potential winner and not just of TV game shows. The potential uses for Watson are many. The system is currently being used to solve very concrete problems in Africa. A delivery service in Lagos, Nigeria, is using the system to improve its logistics.[23]

A good Marvin-type robot could be useful for all kinds of tasks – such as manning call centres and answering users' questions like an actual human. The SmartAction company in Los Angeles has already started doing exactly this. These computers' capacity to learn and recognise natural language is being used to deal with the easiest questions, lightening the load on the flesh-and-blood employees.[24]

The big advantage of using Marvin-type robots in complicated domains like development work or call centres is that they don't get frustrated or depressed, unlike their fictional namesake.

There is no lack of attempts to make computers think like people. Another such project by IBM, christened TrueNorth, tries to move towards human learning. The TrueNorth chip has been modelled on the human brain and consists of 4,096 processor cores simulating a million neurons and 256 million synapses (the two biological building blocks of the human brain)[25]. Like our brains, this chip uses patterns to record data. Real learning, however, involves constantly rewriting the system itself. The smart peopl at IBM are still a long way from figuring out exactly how to do this.

The fifth robot

There is one robot missing from the diagram with the four robots I discuss above: the hybrid man-machine. If you have a pacemaker, you will know what I mean. The fifth robot is a combination of the strong points of man and machine. Science fiction fans will immediately think of cyborgs, cybernetic organisms that improve human beings by adding technology to them. Colour-blind artist Neil Harbisson, for example, has an 'Eyeborg': a device on his head that allows him to feel colours. He is the first person permitted to appear on his passport photograph with such a device.[26] Google created a furore with Google Glass, a pair of spectacles capable of displaying all kinds of information while you look at the world in the normal way – its success was illustrated by the fact that it has since been banned from various cafés in California.

Wearing a Google Glass or having an Eyeborg implanted in your head makes you a cyborg in a pretty literal sense, but this term can also be used figuratively to show how man is becoming closer to technology, and technology closer to man. In their book *The Second Machine Age,* McAfee and Brynjolfsson cite an interesting example of the possibilities of how humans and technology can be combined without scary implants or funny glasses. They talk about a simple chess competition, referring to grand master Garry Kasparov, who was once defeated by the computer Deep Blue. Since then it has become increasingly difficult for a person to beat a computer. The most interesting thing, however, is that at 'freestyle' chess competitions where all types of play are allowed, teams made up of both people and computers often win. While people are better at strategy (creatively thinking ahead), the computer excels in tactics (working out the best move).[27] Thus, a good team with a decent laptop can beat both the most brilliant player and the fastest computer in the world.

A sixth robot?

One last comment before I leave the robots. The diagram with the four quadrants showing Leonardo, Roomba, Jeeves and Marvin is based on an assumption: if we get computers to calculate more and better with ever more data, they will start to resemble us more. Becoming human, however, proves to be a complicated affair.

Dealing with the unexpected requires a few skills that robots just can't seem to get the hang of. For example, robots are still incredibly clumsy if they have to operate in an unknown space (like vacuum cleaner Roomba) while your cat can scout a new room quite fast. Computers remain notoriously bad at pattern recognition. To stick with cats for a moment: the computer system Google Brain has only recently managed to learn how to recognise a cat without being fed rules describing what a cat looks like. Instead, this 'robot' consisting of 16,000 computers was trained using thousands of pictures of cats[28]. A great feat for a computer, but your cat – again – has no such issues. A sixth robot would develop along other lines and could show a different kind of intelligence. A robot that can learn quickly and function with less processing power and less data simply does not yet exist. I would like to stress the 'yet', though, because this could be the next paradigm shift, as referred to by Ray Kurzweil in his predictions for the future. Such sixth robot is outside the scope of this book, as I have chosen to focus on real innovations in the here and now.

Renewal or innovation?

Progress is not just technological advances, and certainly not just about robots. I'd like to broaden the perspective a little and look at the concept of 'innovation'.

If you talk about new things, you often say 'innovation'. This word is often used to describe old wine in new bottles – but fortunately not always. According to Wikipedia, innovation is a new idea, device or process. I would like to tweak this definition just a little: in my opinion, innovation is the application of an idea that can be taken on by others. Ideas in themselves cannot be called innovations: everyone has ideas, but only a few of these manage to actually change society. This can only be done if others see something in your applied idea and run with it. Once again: innovation is not limited to technology. A new form of management can be an innovation. Smart, fast innovation often has both a technical and a social side, as superbly illustrated by the rapid rise of social media. Technology makes interaction possible, and thanks to this people start using the technology in a completely new way, which in turn allows the technology to develop further, and so on.

Technology may also be helpful in gaining insights into how people embrace technology. With its Google Books project, Google has now digitalised thirty million books –

about one quarter of all the books ever published[29]. Erez Aiden has been involved with this project from the start and (with Jean-Baptiste Michel) developed culturonomics, the study of human behaviour and cultural trends on the basis of the use of words. One of the factors making this possible is big data. Aiden and Michel looked at the speed at which innovations penetrate cultures by examining references to new inventions from the beginning of the nineteenth century to the beginning of the twentieth century. They established that new inventions are being taken up increasingly quickly: early nineteenth century, technologies took 65 years to become established. At the beginning of this century, this adoption period had shrunk to just 26 years. Google provides graphs showing how often a word or phrase (an ngram) occurs in all of these publications.

Disruptive innovation

Innovation is most interesting when it leads to a big step forward. I talked above about Ray Kurzweil's paradigm shifts, which were also referred to by Aiden and Michel. Such big changes can be compared with the term 'disruptive innovation' coined by Harvard professor Clayton Christensen. He used this term to distinguish the accompanying innovation from what he calls 'sustaining innovations': innovations that steadily improve the performance of existing products.[30]

Christensen is a professor of business studies. He focusses on very concrete innovations in products and services, rather than grand visions of the future like Ray Kurzweil does. Christensen looks purely at the business aspects of innovations.

Disruptive innovation changes the rules of the game. As a result, it is much more difficult to predict what success it will have. Often, these will be products for which there is not yet a market and for which it is difficult or impossible to carry out accurate market research. This brought Christensen to an interesting insight. In the case of disruptive innovations, the product performance of the new product is often less than that of existing products – at least, in the short term. However, it is often those companies who embrace disruptive innovation that survive.

A good illustration of this phenomenon is the Japanese company Honda, which was enormously successful in Japan in the 1950s with the 'Super Cub': a simple motorcycle that allowed businesses to deliver orders in congested cities. It was also well suited for unpaved roads. It wasn't fast, but very solid. Honda wanted for a long time to break into the American market, as wages were a lot higher there. But there was no market for motorcycles like the Super Cub in the US: on the long American highways, motorcycles had to go far and fast. Honda tried to conquer this new market with a series of models that resembled the American bikes, but at knock-down prices. The bikes proved a false economy: the engines leaked oil and the gearboxes wore out in no time. The company lost a fortune on repairs and flying in new engines from Japan[31]. The Japanese salesmen worked off their frustration by riding the Super Cubs they brought over from Japan off-road in the hills around Los Angeles. Their friends and neighbours saw them having fun on these weird little motorcycles and wanted one too. It was some years before the management in Japan started to grant the many requests to send over Super Cubs from Japan, but once they finally did, the Super Cub became an instant success. It turned out American motorcyclists also enjoyed motocross on a cute, agile little bike; not everyone had to have a big shiny hog for zooming from State to State. The Super Cub became the most-produced motorcycle in history. The American advertising slogan 'You meet the nicest people on a Honda' became a marketing legend.

In 2013, the McKinsey Global Institute published an extensive report on disruptive technologies, applying a more general definition of their disruptive character than Christensen. According to the report's authors, these are technologies with 'the potential to drastically alter the status quo.'[32] They listed twelve technologies that have the most chance of making economic waves in 2025. These are mobile internet, automation of knowledge work, the internet of things, cloud technology, advanced robotics, self-driving cars, genetic research, energy storage, 3D printing, advanced materials, fossil fuels extraction techniques and renewable energy. There are a number of striking things about this selection: energy plays a key role, and Google is involved in one way or another with many of the top twelve. Many of them are also developments in which small companies and individuals can play a significant role. Cloud technology will bring storage closer to everyone and the internet will become increasingly widespread, in terms of the number of devices, the number of people connected and their geographical spread. The institute also believes that consumers will reap the economic fruits of new technologies, as was the case with many other innovations that could be used by everyone, such as steam engines and electricity. According to McKinsey's calculations, two-thirds of the economic surplus from the internet has already trickled down to the consumer – and this is still to happen in relation to mobile internet and the internet of things[33]. They are therefore rather positive about the potential for innovation.

For now, though, the giants still rule. In the field of technology, these include Amazon, Google and Apple. The next chapter deals with them.

3

Big Brother sells you out
On information, big data and privacy

This chapter takes a more detailed look at technology. I will talk about the turbulent development of Apple, Google and Amazon – companies that float on the new, liquid social forces. I will also examine big data: the availability of more and more information and the potential applications and threats this brings. At the end of the chapter, we will be ready to introduce a new organising principle that does justice to technological developments and the potential they offer, but puts people first.

Giants

One of my favourite giants is the BFG, the Big Friendly Giant
created by writer Roald Dahl. At night, the BFG catches sleep-
ing children's dreams and stores them in jars. He returns the
nice dreams to the children and destroys the nightmares.
In a country far away, there are nine other giants who are
even bigger than the BFG – but they are not so friendly and
at night they go out and munch on people. They have names
like Bonecruncher, Maidmasher and Bloodbottler and of
course at the end of the story they come to a sticky end, but
not without the help and wisdom of the little girl Sophie, the
other protagonist in the book. The Queen of England also
plays a role: she sends in the army to overpower the other
giants. I don't want to give too much away, but basically they
live happily ever after.

I would like to focus now on the technology companies
of which I myself am a big customer. They are making use of
innovative possibilities to become a completely new kind of
multinational. They do this by occupying a whole chain within the area of information technology, making social change
possible (for example, by realising social media), squeezing
other players out of the market and making smart use of big
data – the enormous quantities of data now available about
you and me. Are these giants more like the BFG, or more like
a Bonecruncher?

Apple: expansion within the chain

As soon as my first freelance job brought in enough money
to buy my first computer, I bought an Apple, making the
transition from Windows to Mac. My first was a PowerBook
G3 – the last model to be made in sober dark brown. This
decision to switch felt almost like a religious conversion.

Now, when I see other people working on their Apples on the train, for me they still have something of a devout aura about them – I expect I do too. Technology is no longer just a tool, but for a lot of people part of their lifestyle. According to the 2014 Edelman Trust Barometer, people have more confidence in the technology sector than any other business sector.[34]

At the time I switched over, Apple still only made computers. Unlike producers of what at the time were still referred to as 'clones' (Windows-compatible PCs), they provided an operating system. As I described above, Apple is now a jack-of-all-trades or a Very Hungry Caterpillar that builds machines, delivers software, sells music and maintains close control of all these activities. This seems to be the norm for technology companies these days, but it wasn't always like that.

Let's take the case of the PC. IBM introduced the PC in 1981 and conquered a large share of the business market. Quite helpful was the invention of the spreadsheet, which for the first time made it possible to automatically make calculations on one big sheet. This unleashed a revolution in finance departments, including those of small companies. The first spreadsheet programme was called VisiCalc and was made for the Apple II. When Excel appeared in 1986, IBM's PC already had a large market share, and it went on to get even bigger.

But IBM made two big mistakes. The company didn't stake a claim to its own technology. For 100 dollars, you could buy a book explaining the whole architecture of the machine. The result was the proliferation of the 'clones': many different brands of computers, all of which did exactly the same as the more expensive IBM PCs. The second mistake was that IBM didn't want to take over Microsoft. Bill Gates, for a long time the richest person on earth and founder of Microsoft, regularly approached IBM and almost begged them to buy his company. The answer was always no, and because of this

IBM fairly quickly manoeuvred itself out of the PC market. Microsoft's value soon exceeded that of IBM and Microsoft Windows and Microsoft Office made the company the undisputed market leader in operating systems for desktop computers and laptops and for office applications.

At first, Apple also made the mistake of publishing the architecture of its machines. In the 1990s, Apple lost more and more market share to Microsoft. A turning point came with the return of founder Steve Jobs in the early 2000s. Jobs' second tenure brought about computers in candy colours, sleek silver laptops that all creatives wanted, the iPod, the iPhone and the iPad. From a marketing perspective, these were masterstrokes. Don't ask what consumers want, but make something they never even dreamed of, and they come flocking to you in droves.

Even more masterly was Jobs' strategy of taking control of the entire value chain. After controlling both the hardware and the operating system, Apple went further. It started with the iPod and the accompanying iTunes computer application. As gatekeeper, Apple decides whether specific apps will be made available from the Appstore. All the files you want to save for use with your apps are not directly accessible, but can only be accessed through the app. It is a remarkabe development in the history of the computer that users can no longer decide for themswelves what programmes are installed on their computers. (For the record: an iPhone *is* a computer. One that is more than 2,500 times faster than an Apple II from the early 1980s, with tens of thousands of times the internal memory.) A computer has always been a device that receives instructions from its user. It has always been possible to install programmes on a computer and to retrieve data from its memory. But with the iPhone, some of this freedom is lost. Apple manages and controls the software on the iPhone or iPad and wants to know what you plan to do with every single file. It's like buying a car with the bonnet welded shut and a little man standing by the boot. 'No, I'll put your cases in there,' he says. 'Tell me when you want them back.' The computer is no longer completely under your control. Most people don't mind this, as the reduction of freedom comes with a slick and easy-to-use user interface. Nevertheless, it is disconcerting that a large company such as Apple keeps such close tabs on everything, from hardware to data.

In Dutch newspaper NRC of 18 February 2013, Maxim Februari described a similar development when switching to Windows 8. He referred to it as 'share everything, no say.' He makes a comparison with contemporary political developments: when reorganising the structures of the state following conflicts in Iceland and Syria, community sentiments were given precedence over the rights of the individual. In horror, Februari quoted human rights expert Michael Wasco, who opined that the only criterion for the content of a constitution (in this case the Syrian) is whether the constitution is created democratically. Februari's response was: 'Democracy is good, but the rule of law is better.'

I will return to the political implications of not having a say in Chapter 7. For now, I will just admit that Apple has very smartly managed to form a very big chain. All along this value chain, the company itself is now the gatekeeper to the changing middle. As a software developer, for example, you have to dance to Apple's tune if you want your software product to be available on iPhones or iPads. As a user, the same applies: if you want to regain control, you will have to 'jailbreak' your Apple; get round your telephone's operating system and replace it with a hacked version. Alas, if you do this you will no longer receive automatic updates for the operating system, but will have to depend on other hackers for these (unless you are a very good hacker yourself). You will also not have access to the majority of apps. In many ways, your iPhone then becomes an iBrick: a very expensive paperweight.

Google: products as social revolution

Lately, Google has spontaneously begun to offer us all kinds of things, from glasses to e-mail. Google can do a lot, and thanks to Google so can we. 'Yes we can!' they seem to shout out, like Barack Obama – but then he too found out he was more caught up in the framework than he had thought. True, we are not obliged to use all of Google's tools, but we can and so we do – in great numbers. This increase in our range of options brings a restriction: nowadays, we just can't seem to do without them.

Google has for a while now no longer been just a search engine, but rather a more modern version of the TV: the company partly determines what information we have access to. What's more, it's already working on very different products that will tighten its grip on the economy and society, such as glasses, telephones and self-driving cars.

How can we, as individual Davids, defeat this technological Goliath? Do we really have to? In any event, the individual struggles to remain afoot in the economic and technological whirlwind. If the little people can't defeat the giants, the little people and the giants should at least be able to live together in harmony.

The clever thing about Google is that its products look like something that already existed, but in fact are social revolutions in disguise. During these revolutions, significant amounts of power and influence fall to Google rather than to you.

Amazon: benefits of scale

My third example is Amazon. I made my first purchase from this company in the summer of 2001, a game that was sent to me in the old-fashioned form of CD-ROMs. Later that year, I bought the book *Quarterlife Crisis* by Abby Wilner and Alexandra Robbins (which of course in no way reflected my own life at the time).

Amazon started out selling books and some related items. Now, with Kindle, Amazon has a total package consisting of an e-reader, the accompanying software and a whole *digital rights management* system to control the digital rights of makers and publishers, right down to the tiniest detail. In other words: protection against piracy. Less than ten years ago, Amazon also entered the market for the rental of processing capacity and data hosting, just like Google. Amazon is also broadening its field of operations across the whole information chain.

Because the company has such a large market share, a lot of publishers can no longer get by without Amazon. These benefits of scale give Amazon the opportunity to ruthlessly price other intermediaries and suppliers out of the market. The neighbourhood bookshop, which in practice has become a showroom for Amazon (look in the shop, buy from Amazon), is hardly a good business model anymore. In Amazon's business model, the cost of the information remains relatively high, but the added value of the middleman sinks to zero. This is possible thanks to the large scale of the intermediary and the addition of a very different kind of client from the end user: the advertiser. Now compare this with the position of social networking sites: for Facebook, the advertiser is the *only* client of any relevance.

The Economist gave a very apt description of Amazon's ruthless expansion:

> *There is the ability to switch between the real world of atoms and the digital world of bits: Amazon has one of the world's most impressive physical distribution systems, even as it has branched out into cloud computing, e-books, video streaming and music downloads. There is*

the drive for market share over immediate profits. And
there is the slightly creepy feeling that Amazon knows
too much about its users already. So far its insatiable ap-
petite has helped consumers; but as it grows in size and
power the danger is that it will go too far.[35]

In this way, it seems as if Amazon – like Apple – is creating
its very own version of the liquid society. One in which the
physical atoms and the digital bits move freely among one
another, just as long as they are inside the Amazon or Apple
pool. Handy for you and profitable for them, but the question remains: is this the only possible model?

Criticising the giants

The big boys are coming in for a lot of criticism, and not
without reason: particularly in the case of the early technology pioneers, concepts of personal freedom and development
have been rather pushed aside by the interests of big capital.
Communication and information, and with them a significant part of ourselves, are becoming increasingly commercialised.

The Defective by Design campaign focuses on combatting digital rights management. Under the titel 'Amazon
Kindle Swindle' they state that your rights to most e-books
you buy are much more limited than with an old-fashioned
paper book. You can't sell the e-book and the restrictions on
lending it out are extremely severe: this is only possible if you
are an American, the publisher agrees and in any event, you
can do it only once per book. Amazon has already remotely
removed a version of George Orwell's *1984* from Kindle users
because of a rights issue. It is crushingly ironic that the book
in question was this particular one, in which Big Brother
keeps a constant watch over his subjects and freedom has

been eradicated. Amazon as a 'Big Brother' who stops you from putting your e-book in your own virtual bookcase: you are forced to use Amazon's e-reader to read a book you have spent good money on. When you think of all the things you can do with a physical book without fear of sanctions, the sellers of e-books really give you remarkably little freedom. Defective by Design concludes that: 'The Amazon Kindle is an eBook reading computer that poses very serious dangers to society.'[36] Although I use Kindle with a lot of pleasure as an app on my laptop, iPad and telephone, I think we ought to take some of the criticism seriously. Alternatives continue to be more than welcome.

I mentioned above that companies can make huge profits from their benefits of scale and the opportunities to serve a customer other than the consumer: the advertiser. To do this, they have to know everything about you, and sell this information on. This has now been made possible thanks to rapid technological development. Collecting and analysing gigantic quantities of data on just about everything on the planet (and beyond) is not only relevant for companies, but for everyone with an interest in obtaining, increasing or hanging on to power. It's not even that expensive. We will now look at the next big development: big data.

LifeInvader

Big data is by no means just about selling on information on consumers and placing targeted advertisements, although that is one of the most profitable applications, and one that fills newspaper columns.

In Chapter 1, I mentioned the student who requested all the information Facebook had on him and needed a wheel-barrow to carry it all. Since then I have become wary of this social media giant, which in the game *Grand Theft Auto v* is very appropriately called 'LifeInvader'. Facebook is a specialist in big data, passing the 1 billion users mark in 2012; now almost a billion and a half people have a profile. All sorts of things are known about all these people, and this information is the core of Facebook's business model. You are not a customer of Facebook: the customers are the advertisers. In exchange for giving up your data, you get a handy networking tool.

The company Acxiom is not exactly a household name – it is sometimes referred to as the 'biggest company you never heard of.' Nevertheless, this company knows more about you than Facebook or Google. It is the biggest supplier of data on people and companies in the world: with turnover in excess of a billion dollars, the company accounts for slightly more than 10 percent of the services sector in the area of direct marketing.

A report from 2014 by the American Federal Trade Commission investigated this sector and drew up a list of the data on US citizens sold to their clients by the nine biggest suppliers in this area. Taking a look at that list would give you quite a shock.[37] Address, age, gender, citizen service number, driving licence number, income level, loans, bankruptcies, criminal convictions, ethnicity, weight, language, occupation, permits: all this data on just about every American and European citizen is for sale – but it doesn't stop there. In terms of internet use, these companies know how much people like to use Twitter or Facebook, what internet connection they have, how often they google medical information, whether they are members of more than five social networks and whether they upload photos of themselves to these networks. And it goes further still: whether someone has a fireplace, which airline they prefer to use, whether their parents were thrifty, whether they wear contact lenses, whether they are a member of a motorcycle club and whether they collect Elvis Presley memorabilia– Acxiom and its competitors know (or think they know). How much this company knows about me as a citizen of the Netherlands I have no idea – but I do know Acxiom has an office in Amsterdam.

For American citizens, Acxiom has launched an intriguing service: aboutthedata.com. You can log in on this site (with your name, citizen service number, et cetera, because of course they want to know you are who you say you are) and view the personal data they have on you. You can also add to it.

As a citizen of the Netherlands I can't log in on the site, so we will have to rely on reports from American eyewitnesses. At the end of 2013, the boss of Acxiom, Scott Howe, unveiled this new service to a journalist from *The New York Times*.[38] His demonstration quickly revealed that not all the data Acxiom has collected on people is visible. Whether someone has a tendency to gamble or not, for instance, is not shown – although the company can sell that information to interested parties. According to Howe, some items of 'derived data' are not yet on the site, the question is whether these will be put up later. It is quite conceivable that they don't want to give curious citizens too much of a fright. The major data is in any event now visible. Howe thinks consumers will be interested in filling in and improving their own data, and indicating which brands and products interest them. You are going to see advertisements anyway, is their logic, so they might as well be for things that interest you. The best thing, according to the big data boss, will be when consumers can earn credits by keeping their data up-to-date on aboutthedata. com. With these credits they can then shop, for example on Amazon, and the loop is closed.

What is my information worth?

What is all this information on us actually worth? Consultant Eric Siegel, who has written a book on the subject, has estimated this value at about 1,000 Euros per person.[39] In 2013, European Commissioner Viviane Reding estimated the total value of the information on all consumers in the EU at more than 300 billion Euros – a value she says will have trebled by 2020.[40]

More and more is now also known about people other than rich Europeans. In a report from 2012, the World Economic Forum stated that mobile technology in particular offers hope in this respect, 'in part because for many low-income people it is their only form of interactive technology, but it is also easier to link mobile-generated data to individuals. This data can paint a picture about the needs and behaviour of individual users rather than simply the population as a whole', their report 'Big Data, Big Impact' argues.[41] According to this report, every day all kinds of sources, such as online financial transactions, activity on social media and GPS coordinates, generate more than 2.5 trillion (a billion times a billion) bits. They expect the growth of mobile data traffic in the emerging markets (in developing countries) to continue to increase by 100 percent a year for the time being. This opens up a whole range of possibilities: 'By analysing patterns from mobile phone usage, a team of researchers in San Francisco is able to predict the magnitude of a disease outbreak half way around the world. Similarly, an aid agency sees early warning signs of a drought condition in a remote Sub-Saharan region, allowing the agency to get a head start on mobilising its resources and save many more lives.'

Getting creative with big data

How wonderful it is: big data as the philanthropist's best friend. Nevertheless, the first applications have primarily been for profit or cost-savings. To list a few:

- In the retail sector, data is essential for correct pricing. A new phenomenon called dynamic pricing ensures that suppliers can adjust their prices in real time thanks to computer systems that get information from big data which, according to *The Financial Times*, delivers a lot of information to investors and entrepreneurs.[42] Amazon also analyses other suppliers' prices, and makes sure it stays below these.

- Big data proves to be a useful tool for telemarketing. The company Beyond Verbal analyses emotions on the basis of voice intonation using an algorithm based on big data. In a brilliant video clip used by the company in one of its advertising campaigns, the emotions analysed are shown next to an interview with Steve Jobs, already sick, who talks about the development of the iPad.

- The financial services sector can improve its services by using big data. Companies such as LendUp and Climate Corporation analyse weather patterns to determine the price of insurance for agricultural crops. They carry out simulations using technology specifically intended to be used with large amounts of data.[43] Big data also plays an increasingly decisive role in granting credit. This is true for start-up Wonga, which lends small amounts for a maximum of one month at an extremely high rate of interest, a modern pawn shop, but with your data as security. It's not just small startups: the whole industry is involved. As Francisco González said in *The Financial Times*: 'A new financial ecosystem is being created. In two decades, we will go from 20,000 "analogue" banks today worldwide to no more than several dozen "digital" banks. Diverse niche businesses will exist, but most will be mere "suppliers" for the much-reduced number of digital banks acting as "knowledge distributors."' [44]

- Huge advances can be made in the care sector using big data. Since 2014, ios (the operating system of the iPad and iPhone) has featured a health app which brings together all the data on your own health. If you were to combine all this individual data (and who knows, maybe this is already happening), you would have a database that could tell you a lot about the health of the population, and maybe save huge amounts of money as well. IBM is already experimenting in this area with its Watson project: the system is sometimes able to come up with expected diagnoses based on medical examinations and files. [45] Storing, sharing and processing medical data is a very sensitive subject for reasons of privacy. Electronic health records, in which care providers can record all data on their patients, is undoubtedly a good idea from the point of view of efficiency and transparency, but politically it is something of a nightmare. Nevertheless, big data now seems crucial to research into new medicines, the evaluation of treatment methods and preventive health care. Google boss Larry Page has said in an interview that Google does not use data on the health of its users, but: 'If we did we'd probably save 100,000 lives next year.' [46] I think he is right, although I prefer him not to offer my medical records to the highest bidder.

- Data is power, so politics is never far away. It has frequently been stated that Barack Obama became president thanks to his use of big data. His campaign used Acxiom to find promising *swing voters* using a tool called VoteBuilder. Volunteers in safe states (where the Democrats were guaranteed a win) then descended on the swing states to set up a campaign of 'organised stalking on a gigantic scale' as one volunteer called it. [47] If you can see on your tablet exactly whose door you are knocking on or who you are calling, you can choose your 'victims' in a much more targeted manner, and then convince them using tailor-made arguments. One minor problem with this approach was that some people were approached very, very frequently. One person recorded a voicemail message saying: 'I'm a Democrat, I already voted and I'm a volunteer with the campaign.'[48]

- Use of big data within the energy sector is increasing. In January 2014 it was announced that Nest, the maker of smart thermostats, had been bought by Google for more than 3 billion dollars.[49] The numbers don't lie, so it's extremely useful to collect big data to make households aware of their energy consumption (and draw more general conclusions). Big data is used even more extensively in the production of energy. IBM supplies services to the oil industry to allow research, extraction, refining and global operations to run more efficiently.[50] The open-source platform Apache Hadoop, which is capable of processing terabytes of data, is also a useful tool for the oil giants. The company MapR supplies services on this platform ranging from searching for oil to protecting oil platforms against terrorist attacks. The recognition of patterns in all the available data is worth billions. Extracting oil and gas continue to require massive investment, but thanks to big data Shell and Esso are able to use these natural resources more and more efficiently, and are exposed to fewer risks.[51]

Data is the new oil

'Data is the new oil' is a much-heard comment in the corridors of the European Commission, the lounges of the tech companies in Silicon Valley, the boardrooms of Unilever and

Shell and hopefully also in meeting chamber of the Dutch
Council of Ministers. And little wonder: this is a raw material available in ever larger quantities at an ever lower price,
which we are learning to refine better all the time and for
which more and more applications are being found.

As I have shown above, oil and data are a happily married
couple. In linguistic terms, this is true as well. If you enter
the words 'data' and 'oil' in Google Ngram Viewer, you can
see how 'data' started to overtake the word 'oil' as early as
the beginning of the 1950s, continuing to rise rapidly into the
1980s (Figure 3.1). Now, both words maintain a fairly constant presence in writing.[52]

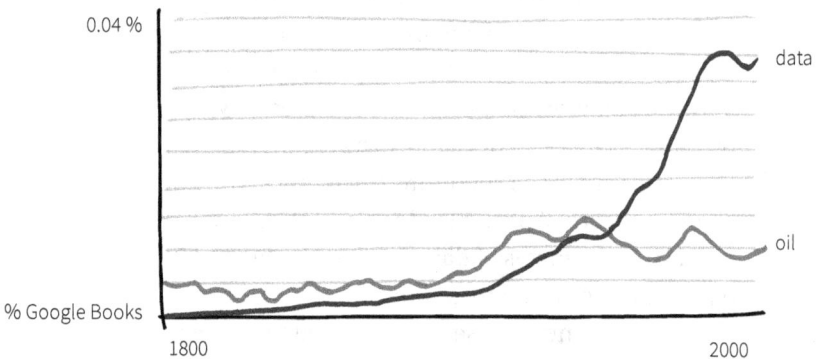

Figure 3.1

Whether oil refineries will still exist in fifty years' time remains to be seen, but I don't doubt that companies working
in the field of Acxiom today, will still be around.

The traditional production factors – necessary to create
value – used to be land, capital and labour. Some people are
saying that information has now become one of these. In any
case, the influence of land and labour have waned. Brian
Gentile, a technology entrepreneur, believes that the major
production factors alongside capital have become information and time. He has written in *Forbes*: 'Success in the new

economic battleground is based on our differential use of time and information, the two new factors of production. Because we can have no more of the former and an unlimited amount of the latter, our need for efficiency is never-ending.'[53]

Other views

Not everyone believes in the promise of big data. Nassim Taleb, who we met in the first chapter, refers to this as a big lie and is annoyed by the hype that seems to surround the term. He said in an interview: 'In a hospital in Toronto they examined patient data over a period of 28 years. Guess what? The duration of the hospitalization showed a correlation with the constellation of the patient. Why? The more data you explore, the more patterns you think you discover, but that are pure coincidence and also do not repeat. People who love Big Data are either not scientists, or they can profit from it. The whole idea is bullshit.'[54]

I take this comment with a pinch of salt. If big data were just nonsense, the industry that has grown up around it wouldn't be able to make such huge profits. It is good to look at the limitations of big data, however. That word 'big' transforms data into something very different from the traditional information used by the traditional archivist or academic.

I would like to briefly mention three challenges from the book by Erez Aiden and Jeap-Baptiste Michel, the inventors of culturomics.[55] One challenge is that big data is structured very differently from the data academics usually come across. A second is that big data doesn't easily fit the traditional scientific method. This is exactly what Taleb means: when *mining* big data, there is often no hypothesis set up in advance – as it should be – but rather the researchers (or computer programmes) just randomly start seeing what connections can be made. A third challenge is where the data can be found: 'As scientists, we are used to getting data by experimenting in our laboratories or going out into the natural world to write down our observations. Getting data is, to some extent, within the scientist's control. But in the world of big data major corporations – and even governments – are often the gatekeepers of the most powerful datasets. And they, their citizens, and their customers care a great deal about how the data is used.' These two researchers, curious as they are, see this mostly as a major obstacle.

In addition, I am quite concerned about what happens to my data, particularly when it is in the hands of giant technology companies such as Google and Facebook, who have based their whole business model around free information and big data as a source of income. I have my reservations about making use of all kinds of free services and giving up my privacy in the process. And I'm certainly not alone in this. The Dutch initiative Qiy carried out a survey and found that 85 percent of people in the Netherlands would like to retain control of the databases in which information on them is stored.[56] Qiy gives you the option to determine through its website what data you share, for example, when you buy a bicycle online. You can temporarily take this data out of your 'information locker', then when you've completed the purchase, your locker closes again. A very healthy development, in my opinion.

Information expert and artist Jaron Lanier is not enthusiastic about the technology giants who give away information to users for free, while their real clients are the companies who can convert this data into profits. According to Lanier, this is leading to an impoverishment of our economy it is unlikely to survive. He writes: 'Making information free is survivable so long as only limited numbers of people are disenfranchised. As much as it pains me to say so, we can survive if we only destroy the middle classes of musicians, journalists, and photographers.'[57]

He believes we should retake possession of our own data. Only if we can let go of the idea of free information we can create a real, growing information economy with a new middle class. He is pinning his hopes on a form of micro-payments to reward people for the use of their data – whether this is the personal information you place on a social media site or a witty remark you make in a blog or a book.

With this thought in mind, Acxiom's website aboutthedata.com is maybe not such a bad idea – with their system, that allows you to earn points for completing the data in their database, they at least give something back to the user.

In Chapter 6 I will look at innovative new ways to create value in the liquid society, bearing in mind Jaron Lanier's interesting and useful idea.

Forwards

Big data is not infallible. It is, as has been commented in Dutch newspaper NRC *Handelsblad*, 'not so much looking for a needle in a haystack, but rather using a whole haystack to find a needle. This is useful in an era when companies and other bodies are collecting large quantities of data and want to analyse this.'[58] Very useful, but you do end up with some pretty weird needles. At the first ever presentation of aboutthedata.com, it turned out that Acxiom founder Scott Howe's file contained incorrect data. I downloaded my personal archive from Facebook, in which you can see your Ads Topics, things Facebook associates with you. A lot of these were relevant, but since I don't watch football, the term 'Forward (Association Football)' came as something of a surprise to me. Nevertheless, I quite like the term 'forward' – we have to move forward, and quickly too, and not be too defensive about it. Big data is here to stay: an essential component of a liquid society characterised by radical transparency and radical decentralisation.

4

The diopticon
A new view of social relations

*In the previous two chapters, I looked at technological inno-
vation, big data and the development of the large companies
who use these to their benefit. In this chapter, I will describe a
new model for looking at reality that has been made possible
by these developments: the diopticon, which allows everyone
to see everyone else. I will examine practical applications of
this model and describe some real consequences and challenges.*

Instead of searching the web, now you go to SeeChange, you type
in Myanmar. Or you type in your high school boyfriend's name.
Chances are there's someone who's set up a camera nearby,
right? Why shouldn't your curiosity about the world be rewarded?
You want to see Fiji but can't get there? SeeChange. You want to
check on your kid at school? SeeChange. This is ultimate trans-
parency. No filter. See everything. Always.

Dave Eggers, *The Circle*

The panopticon: power lies with the watchman

Have you ever had the feeling you're locked up in a prison?
That the reality you see around you is not real but that others,
who you can't see, are exercising huge but subtle power over
you? Then you may be stuck in a panopticon.

The panopticon is, in its most concrete sense, a prison
that was never built – at least, not exactly as originally envisaged by its inventor, Enlightenment philosopher Jeremy
Bentham (1748-1832). He described the concept in 1791, and
subsequently made great efforts to get his design realised.
With much difficulty he obtained a piece of land on which
the prison could be built. He probably envisaged becoming
the governor of the new institution himself. It all came to
nothing: after more than twenty years of conflict, the British
parliament decided to return the plot of land to the government.

Bentham may have gained some satisfaction in hindsight:
the great philosopher Michel Foucault elevated the panopticon to a pregnant metaphor for power relations within
contemporary society. What's more, some actual prison
buildings have been built that resemble his model, such as

the Panóptico de Cundinamarca in Bogotá, Colombia, now
a museum, and Prison Pentridge near Melbourne, Austra-
lia. Bentham had great plans for the panopticon: 'Morals
reformed – health preserved – industry invigorated – instruction diffused – public burthens lightened – Economy seated,
as it were, upon a rock – the Gordian knot of the Poor-Laws
are not cut, but untied – all by a simple idea in Architecture!'[59] In spite of Bentham's lofty social ambitions, I'd like
to concentrate here on the design in its original function.
The panopticon ('all seeing' in Greek) is built in a circle. The
cells containing the prisoners are located around the outer
wall. In the centre is a watchman. He can see all inmates,
but they can see neither him nor their peers. The prisoners
are objects rather than subjects (they are the watched) and
are isolated individuals (they have contact with no one else).
Power is therefore entirely asymmetric, and lies fully with
the watchman. He doesn't need to watch everyone all the
time, because the prisoners can't see him. Thus, they will
behave as if they could be observed at any moment, without
the need to apply further coercion or pressure. Power is con-
tinuously present in a virtual way, even though its presence
is primarily in the prisoner's head. Discipline and order
flourish in the penal establishment.

Panopticon

Figure 4.1

According to Bentham, the panopticon model could also work well in hospitals or schools: in a hospital, the patients would not infect one another and in school, the pupils would not be able to copy from one another.

The panopticon instils fear: the watchman's ability to see all around has an oppressive effect. In his novel *1984*, George Orwell described a dystopia that is the result of an all-seeing, unknown power: a complete lack of freedom in the face of an omnipresent, totalitarian state.

Our society has quite a few panoptical characteristics. There are cameras on the streets and in buildings; these days, these increasingly take the form of an opaque hemisphere on the ceiling, so that it's impossible to know which way the camera is pointing. Combine this technology with the 'internet of things', support from big data and super-fast computers and you wouldn't need anyone except a high-profile data analyst and the odd watchman to keep tabs on an enormous physical space. The surveillance model in which the elite *could* watch at any given moment (but doesn't have to) could be perfected into a situation in which the elite can watch now or later, thanks to cheap storage of all data.

We know for sure that this is possible and that it is happening, but we don't know exactly who or what organisation or body is watching, reading or listening to what, or when. As a result, people are cautious and anxious. The former could be seen as an improvement; the second not so much. Now, in the face of scandals revealing that the government are collecting much more data than was initially intended, emotions are running high. When, in 2012, it turned out that the Dutch government had passed on 18 million phone records to the Americans, The Dutch were shocked – not only because it had happened, but also because it was *possible*. The next time, the effect will be lessened – particularly if a terrorist attack has taken place or has been prevented, a situation that provides the government with an argument in favour of the panopticon. Personally, I don't know which I am more afraid of: terrorism, the all-seeing government or the citizenry of a democratic society so worn down and demoralised they are willing to let the government do whatever it likes.

These critic remarks follow the thought of French philosopher Michiel Foucault, who popularised Bentham's term and explained it in terms of crushing power. He discusses this in more detail in his book *Surveiller et punir*, translated into English as *Discipline and Punish: The Birth of the Prison*. It is not so much how power is managed through legal structures. Rather, the ability of the elite to organise this in everyday practice determines the actual relations that govern people's behaviour. Power is exercised more subtly, more covertly, by disciplining the masses through the unwritten rules of the game which are determined by the elite.

It's not just about cameras and monitoring the internet. The hierarchy, the rituals and the movements in everyday life, the rigid subdivision of time and the bond to particular places are important. As to the last thing mentioned, a nomadic lifestyle is the first thing those in power try to deny to normal citizens, since they need to know where their citizens are. Bureaucratic rules and statistics serve the panopticon because they are able to objectify individuals, separately and in groups: after all, a statistical group doesn't talk back, but you can reach it through policies. A rigid bureaucracy renders power opaque.

Our daily lives are full of techniques used to discipline us: timesheets in the office, working nine till five, the school bell, having to register with the local authority and the very literal surveillance on the streets. In the city of Edinburgh, Scotland, you can be reprimanded for dropping litter on the ground by a loudspeaker built into the security cameras. And maybe the police are watching you too.

Foucault died in 1984. At that time, the French had Minitel, a precursor to the internet that worked through the telephone network and was one of the first widely used ICTs in Europe. The philosopher, who died way too young, would no doubt have wanted to dedicate an article to this; I wonder how he would have explained this development in terms of power relations. Unlike how the internet is constructed now, with Minitel you used a terminal and a telephone to log in to a central server. Because of the existence of this central server, Minitel was like a kind of new, electronic panopticon. But it also provided a glimpse of the potential to break out of the panopticon: Minitel was interactive. It led to new exchanges, both vertically (between the service and the user) and horizontally (between users).

I would like to add two more interactions to the model of the panopticon. Following others, I refer to the first of these – between the few and the many – as the synopticon. Then, I will then describe an interaction between the many and the many, which I refer to as the diopticon, a term that, to the best of my knowledge, is new.

The panopticon revised

The panopticon is a mind-set that explains how an elite can exert power over the masses in subtle and not so subtle ways. Nevertheless, these masses look back, and this too exerts power. This has always been the case, but technological developments and mobility make this possible at an ever quicker pace. The rigid panopticon, based on a sedentary society has not disappeared, but now has to tolerate other power structures alongside it – sometimes these even overshadow it. Before coming to my own model, I will discuss Zygmunt Bauman's post-panopticon and the synopticon proposed by the Norwegian Thomas Mathiesen.

Zygmunt Bauman believes that the panopticon is losing importance in our liquid modernity: 'What matters in
post-Panoptical power-relations is that the people operating
the levers of power on which the fate of the less volatile part-
ners in the relationship depends can at any moment escape
beyond reach – into sheer inaccessibility.'[60] This means
the end of 'mutual involvement' of the watchman and the
watched which not only keeps the watched in their place,
but also restricts the freedom of movement of the watchman. The relations between capital and labour, leaders and
followers, commanders and troops are becoming slippery
and making way for 'escape, slippage, elision and avoidance,
the effective rejection of any territorial confinement with
its cumbersome corollaries of order-building, order-main-
tenance and the responsibility for the Top of Formconse-
quences of it all as well as of the necessity to bear their costs.'

Bauman illustrates the latter – the tendency of the
post-panopticon to tear down walls – with the Gulf Wars and
the conflict in the former Yugoslavia, where the old objective
of warfare, to conquer land, was replaced with a hit-and-run
strategy aimed at breaking down the walls put up by local
warlords. The reason for this was simply that these walls
were an obstacle to global free trade – the real reason for
intervention. I have trouble with this argument: it is the governments who try to force us to remain 'sedentary' as much
as possible; to stay in one place, making us easy to find. Land
still represents value, and therefore power. Therefore, it is not
the watchman but the watched who are constantly proving
to be slippery. I experience this myself as a global traveller
and writer: I like to stray from the beaten track, even though
at times this means I have to subject myself to strange pan-
optica.

In addition to the physical aspect, Bauman emphasises
another aspect that I agree with: repression has to a significant extent made way for seduction. In his words: 'Spec-

tacles take the place of surveillance without losing any of the disciplining power of their predecessor. Obedience to standards (a pliable and exquisitely adjustable obedience to eminently flexible standards, let me add) tends to be achieved nowadays through enticement and seduction rather than by coercion – and it appears in the disguise of the exercise of free will, rather than revealing itself as an external force.'[61] The desire expressed by politicians to reduce the 'gap between citizens and politicians' can be seen in this light: in the old, rigid social order you never heard such a thing. In the liquid society, those in power have to use a new bag of tricks – something governments are not always successful at. Town-hall meetings usually attract the usual suspects; election turnouts are dwindling and parties that oppose the established order are gaining in popularity.

Huge technological giants such as Amazon and Facebook, which I discussed in the previous chapter, are much better at using this new, liquid way of exercising power. After all, seduction is their core business; if making advertising for companies on these platforms pays, these companies can make a profit.

In the post-panopticon, the government reduces the citizen to a customer but remains relatively powerless; new global platforms further reduce the customer to an object to be seduced and, if this works out, to be sold to the highest bidder.

The above can be seen as a lamentation of the new power relations, but there is hope: the masses are looking back at the old watchman. The roles are being reversed.

The synopticon: the watchman being watched

In 1997, Norwegian sociologist Thomas Mathiesen came up with a complement to Bentham and Foucault's panopticon.

Alongside the panopticon, in which a few watch the many, he also sees a 'synopticon', in which the many watch a few. He held that the rise of the bourgeoisie and the advent of modern panoptic power techniques at the beginning of the nineteenth century, was accompanied by the rise of the mass media. The first newspapers appeared roughly at the moment the principles of freedom, equality and fraternity were committed to paper. Now, there are no more public executions to underline where power lies, but we have much naming and shaming in the newspapers.[62] Thus, Mathiesen's synopticon features an interaction: the few watch the many, and vice versa (see Figure 4.2).

Mathiesen attaches great importance to the traditional mass media; after all, he was writing in 1997. This perhaps is why he misses the point that the most important transformation of the panopticon is not the change in the direction of watching, but the interaction that arises between the few and the many. The masses looked at the elite even before everyone was parked in front of the TV. The synopticon, in my definition, the two-way process of influence between the masses and the elite, has now acquired a powerful set of instruments on the side of the masses. Everyone is now armed with a mobile telephone, uses it for recording and shares the results online – in any event, the few must fear for their privacy. Internet is awash with sex tapes of the stars and private confessions by politicians. Names and reputations are made and broken in an instant.

The synopticon is not just about images in a literal sense; it is also interesting from other perspectives. An online citizens' panel that provides advice to a local politician on neighbourhood matters and monitors how these are dealt with in practice exercises soft pressure from the large group onto the small circle in power (and sometimes on individuals).

Synopticon

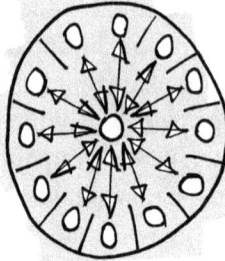

Figure 4.2

There can be little doubt that power constantly seeks new forms. Power also has a tendency to concentrate, and people and organisations will continue to try to gain more of it. It is becoming increasingly difficult for the few to get the many to dance to their tune using traditional tools of power. Reality is becoming more diffuse (or liquid); the decreasing importance of physical place due to virtualisation undermines the effectiveness of the old, powerful position in the middle. It's no coincidence that the tools used by the few resemble the tools used by the many. With our smartphones, each of us carries around an espionage device that would have made the Stasi of the former East Germany green with envy. The speed at which innovations like mobile telephone and Facebook are accepted by the general public underlines various human needs: to renew and to belong, but also to be in charge of our own lives.

The diopticon: everyone can see everything

I would like to suggest an alternative. Although the panopticon and the synopticon will not disappear completely – and certainly not any time soon – there is room for a new arrangement. I call this the diopticon: the many watching the many. The Greek prefix *dia-* means completely, through, by

means of and this emphasises the importance of the connections between individuals and thus the power of the individual – or rather his possibilities to add value to the world
around him.

Seeing still plays a role: the many see the many.

In a diagram, it looks like this.

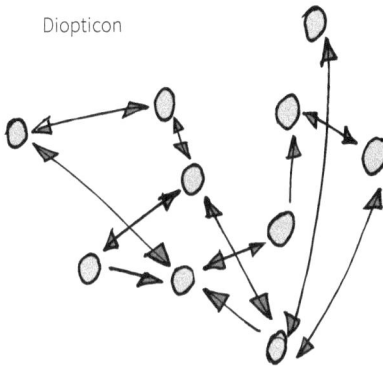

Diopticon

Figure 4.3

This diopticon has a number of interesting characteristics; I
will discuss five of these below.

1. The power of connections

The change a diopticon can bring about is more about the
connections than about the individuals themselves. Connections can easily be made and just as easily broken.

When value is added in the diopticon, various new
connections are made, old ones broken and useful existing
ones activated. In line with Foucault's approach, you could
also describe the addition of value as the exercise of power
and influence within our own environment – whatever you
choose to call it, the consequences can be quite modest and
in everyone's interest: a new idea for an innovative, sustain-

able business getting support through crowdsourcing, or booking a trip on a website after reading reviews by others who have been there.

When talking about a network, we often think of a collection of points linked together – these points could be computers, or we ourselves and the people we know. This sounds very plausible, and for a long time this has been the main academic definition. However, a better method has been suggested for making meaningful statements about the functioning of networks. In 2010, researchers Ahn, Bagrow and Lehmann published a fascinating article in *Nature* in which it is not the nodes in the network, but the connections that populate the communities. They applied this not only to networks of people, but also to biochemical networks describing the interactions between proteins.[63] This approach proved effective in picking out the relevant communities, particularly in the case of strongly overlapping networks.

In order to examine the function and strength of communities, we therefore need to shift our focus. It's not who's looking at Facebook that counts, but the friend requests accepted, the likes and the shared membership of a page. At a party, what's relevant is not who is there, but who clinks glasses with whom.

2. Less location-specific

In the diopticon, connections are less and less about location. In fact, you could even say that, in a diopticon, at any given moment you can be everywhere at once. This could be in a very literal sense (on Facebook, Dordrecht is just as far away as Timbuktu), but also figuratively: a small social entrepreneur can operate simultaneously in Amsterdam, throughout Europe and at a global scale. In *Liquid Modernity*, Bauman describes how he was sitting waiting with his wife at the airport for their flight to depart. He saw two men busily making phone calls and using their laptops. They weren't talking to one another, but very much with others. Nevertheless, they were acutely aware of one another:

> 'As a matter of fact, it was the awareness of that presence which seemed to motivate their actions. The two men were engaged in competition – as intense, frenzied and furious as competition could be. Whoever finished the cellular conversation while the other was still talking, searched feverishly for another number to press; clearly the number of connections, the degree of 'connectedness,' the density of the respective networks which made them into nodes, the quantity of other nodes they could link to at will, were matters of utter, perhaps even superior, importance to both: indices of social standing, position, power and prestige. Both men spent that hour and a half in what was, in its relation to the airport bar, an outer space.'[64]

Bauman's observation demonstrates several things:
- You are who you know: the connections within your network determine your status and effectiveness.
- The speed at which you can (and often have to) switch within that network is extremely high.
- The physical surroundings are less important in this respect than they used to be.
- These physical surroundings are not irrelevant, however, as we still travel and will continue to do so in search of authentic, first-hand experiences.

The distinction between online and offline is also blurring, and not only in terms of technology, as has been shown by Spanish sociologist Manuel Castells: 'All the studies on the internet show that people who are more social on the internet are also more social face-to-face.'[65] Just imagine a school class, for example. Who are the kids in contact with the whole time online? Exactly – the same people they sit next to all day in school. The more active they are and the bigger their network is, the more active they will also be in real life. The more the liquid society permeates school, the more the class will lose its importance as a physical space: you don't need to constantly cram pupils into classrooms together in groups of 25 when you can make connections in a dynamic, ad hoc way.

The world has changed since I addressed a letter to myself at school, writing my name, house number, street, city, province, country, continent and then 'The Earth' at the bottom, in the usual rigid hierarchy. The world shown by the diagram Figure 4.4 is hardly relevant anymore.

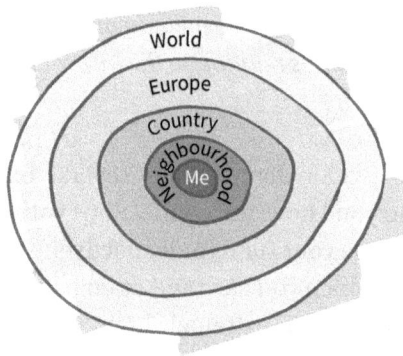

Figure 4.4

At a meeting in Brussels in July 2014, I also had this insight in relation to the European Union. It's incredibly old-fashioned to talk about the division of tasks between the EU and the Member States, as if they constitute some kind of hierarchical structure. Problems get solved by tackling them together. It is only possible to add value in a liquid society by allowing different levels to merge in a dynamic way. I will discuss this in greater detail in Chapter 7.

It is possible to draw a second version of the diopticon (Figure 4.5), which does justice to both the interaction between the parts (you and I) and the big pan on the stove in which these parts are freely moving. Identities and perspectives meet and merge. I will return to this in Chapter 7, in which I will look more intensively at the concept of power.

Diopticon

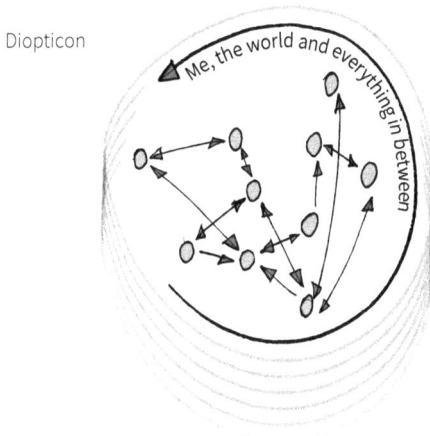

Me, the world and everything in between

Figure 4.5

3. Time as a decisive factor

Location plays such a minor role thanks to the incredible speed at which interactions take place, such as the spread of news. In Chapter 2, I wrote about Moore's law; the pace is getting quicker all the time. In the liquid society, change will remain the norm. The parts move freely and quickly in the liquid; connections between these parts are established and dissolved just as quickly. Change is the only constant factor.

Time plays an increasingly decisive role here. Bauman rightly states that solid substances neutralise time, while time is a major factor for liquid substances.[66] In other words: while the panopticon captures time by structuring it and dividing it up it into schedules and deadlines, the diopticon is all about dynamics and acceleration.

In an economic sense, the concept of time is undergoing a significant development. The industrial revolution marked the first occasion when a worker's time was directly related to his output. Over the decades, the worst excesses of exploiting workers were scaled back somewhat: working hours were reduced and subjected to statutory maximums; child labour was abolished below a certain age and education made compulsory (based of course on a clear timetable) with the aim of emancipating the masses. This industrial model of work characterised externally by time schedules, collective bargaining and clocking in and out and with labour productivity as the dominant norm, still exists today. In a well-functioning diopticon, however, time is not a rigid construct, but something we can regain. More so than in the past, we can now invest time ourselves and multiply it by handing over tasks to others, or to algorithms. It is no longer necessary for us all to pretend we are an average human being, at our most effective when we work from nine to five, five days a week at a desk, with seven and a half hours' sleep a day. Time is coming down from its ivory tower and becoming a decentralised concept, depending on the context. One size does not fit all.

4. Radically decentralised

That last statement doesn't only apply to time. With the melting of the pyramid we have set up in modern life, other aspects of the economy, society and our private lives are democratising and decentralising as well.

The diopticon is radically decentralised: the emphasis is not on any central function or vertical structure. No wonder: as in a liquid, 'top' and 'bottom' are of little relevance, hierarchy and the liquid society are an ill match.

Although the need for connections is great, the traditional ways of establishing them are in need of renewal. The role of the intermediary is no longer naturally in the hands of a single party. The moving parts prefer to find their own way, and make connections where necessary. You and I can step into the diopticon at any moment and play the role of middleman. A handy application of technology can do this too.

This leads to a situation in which a lot of problems can be solved by an individual or a small group. For example, you can become an energy supplier by selling the wattage you generate on your exercise bike to the grid. You can even set up a power company with a few friends, like four young entrepreneurs in the Netherlands did, without large investments and within a year, under the name Vandebron (Dutch for 'from the source').

5. Radically transparent

The diopticon is radically transparent – otherwise it couldn't function and would seize up. For the right connections to be made, individuals must be able to see who has what to offer and when. (The model is an '-opticon' after all.) Both society and technological developments exert pressure to make the world transparent.

I had my first real eye-opener on this topic in 2010. I wondered aloud in a tweet which of two hotels in Hangzhou, China, I should choose. A few hours later I got a reply. Not from one of my Twitter followers, but directly from one of the hotels I had mentioned. 'We are very pleased you are thinking of staying with us. If you have any questions, please do hesitate to contact us.' I didn't hear anything from the other hotel, so the choice was easily made.

Not all companies realise how important transparency can be and how they can make use of this. In 2013, British Airways had a public relations disaster. Hasan Syed, furious about the manner in which the company had dealt with his father's lost luggage, sent out a tweet. To make things worse, he spent 1,000 dollars to make it a promoted tweet, so that it reached people who were not following him. British Airways didn't pick up on this until nine hours later, as their communication department works from nine to five (rather strange for a company that operates all over the world). By then, 76,000 people had seen the message and the media had run with it.

In these early days of the diopticon, it is mainly individuals who are consciously and transparently swimming around in the liquid. The system of government bodies and established interests is still resisting strongly. Not everywhere, mind you. In Norway, as I mentioned above, the law requires that all tax returns are public. No whistle-blowers are needed to hack into this data and publish it – it's already in the public domain. This does reduce to citizens' fiscal privacy to zero, but in all transparency and openness, this is how the Norwegians decided to do things.

The dystopian diopticon

At the beginning of this chapter, I quoted from Dave Eggers' critical novel *The Circle*. As George Orwell gives the ultimate dystopian version of the panopticon in his novel *1984*, in *The Circle* Eggers sketches the most nightmarish vision of the diopticon imaginable. At the beginning of the book, set in the very near future, Mae Holland gets a highly sought-after job with The Circle, a huge company that resembles a combination of Facebook and Google. 'The Circle' is responsible for trail-blazing innovations that turn social interaction upside down: with SeeChange, millions of portable cameras film 24/7 and politicians feel forced to exercise total transparency. The need to be constantly in contact with people, familiar and strangers puts Mae and everyone else under intense pressure. The company's slogans are pretty blatant: *Secrets are lies*; *Sharing is caring*; *Privacy is theft*.[67] With these, Eggers pays tribute to George Orwell, who used similar slogans in his dystopia: *War is Peace*; *Freedom is Slavery*; *Ignorance is Strength*. *The Circle* is an ominous book, in which all aspects of the diopticon I referred to above take on such extreme forms it is in danger of exploding. Every week, a new screen with even more interaction and information is added to Mae's workstation. Privacy no longer exists as the company sets a course for the ominous 'closing of the circle'. If you want to know what that means, you'll have to read the book.

Although well-written, contemporary and highly relevant, *The Circle* doesn't shy away from exaggeration. In reality, the diopticon is not developing quite that quickly, and other views are not so mercilessly dismissed. Also, the system won't allow itself to be pushed aside or replaced that easily by technology companies.

First, I would like to look at a few forms the diopticon is taking in our current everyday practice. Later in this chapter, and in the book, I will discuss the conditions that can help us keep the diopticon useful and acceptable.

I will also discuss some more examples of and ideas about the operation of the diopticon in practice. I will start from a more obvious perspective: technology. Then I will take a broader view, although technology will remain present in the background.

Internet: decentralised functions

The internet is organised along the lines of a diopticon: packages of information find their own way to a random destination somewhere else in the network. This happens at great speed and also transparently: in principle all these packages can be examined by every node they pass through.

Exceptions to this are conceivable. Encryption techniques are among the strategies to mask this transparency. Applications that allow the internet to work optimally, such as peer-to-peer technology, show that every computer in addition to a sender and an addressee can above all also be a link in the network: from this the technology derives its strength.

Some central functions and services exist on the internet, such as the registry of names and related IP addresses. This information is essential for all users and is stored in multiple copies throughout the network.

The virtual currency bitcoin does a similar thing using the 'block chain', the virtual cash register which records who owns each bitcoin and who previously owned it. Every bitcoin user has a copy of this file, which is an essential part of the virtual wallet.

Wikipedia: liquid knowledge

The Wikipedia online encyclopaedia shows that transparency is a precondition for the quality of an online encyclopaedia to which everyone can contribute. The first person to compile an encyclopaedia, Enlightenment thinker Denis Diderot, would probably have had his doubts about Wikipedia. The idea of 'power to the people', radical as it may have been in the day, was being expressed and shaped by a progressive elite. Diderot wrote quite a bit of his encyclopaedia himself and edited the rest with his colleague d'Alembert. Diderot's work proved controversial because his ideas about religious tolerance, democracy and freedom of expression represented a threat to the aristocratic elite. Consequently, he has entered the history books as a major exponent of the Radical Enlightenment. According to Diderot, everyone has the right to doubt everything – a bold statement in an extremely god-fearing era. 'Scepticism is the first step towards truth,' Diderot wrote in his *Philosophical Thoughts*.

The second step is abolition of the hierarchy – which has now happened with great consistency in Wikipedia. As a dioptical reinvention of Diderot's encyclopaedia, Wikipedia is radically decentral: everyone is allowed to contribute, and many people actually do it. *'Power to the people'* has become a reality in a liquid context of constantly changing networks, with a huge reservoir of liquid knowledge.

The liquid good cause

Good causes have long been claimed by a large number of organisations and individuals acting as intermediaries. We outsourced our conscience, as it were. There didn't use to be many opportunities to personally combat hunger in Africa, or these were inefficient. You could only really do so through the government, or organisations like Oxfam, Red Cross or Amnesty International, big 'black boxes' that were far from transparent in their operations. They looked to you (i.e.: begged for money) and acted as an intermediary in the chain of charity.

The last decade or so have brought many changes. Through the 1%Club, Dutch citizens can donate money to small initiatives and follow the results on Facebook; the Danish platform MyC4 does the same, but by way of micro-investments in small businesses in developing countries. Crowdfunding and crowdsourcing are setting the pace. This way, generous donors or micro-venture capitalists have the opportunity to contribute more than just money. For example, they can add extra value to their investments by using their networks, and so contribute 'social capital': adding connections to the liquid soup.

The poorest continent offers the most opportunities. The problem was (and still is, in many places) a lack of infrastructure. If you design a new one, you can set it up in a different way. One positive example for a dioptical future is the fact that, in Africa, the development of a landline network for fixed telephony has been completely skipped in favour of mobile technology. The latter is location-independent, dynamic, fast and scaleable. It merges people and their devices for communication.

Thanks in part to such developments, social enterprise Moyee Coffee ('radically good coffee') goes much further than offering a fair price for its raw materials ('fair trade'). This young, Dutch company thinks that doesn't go far enough, and strives for fairness throughout the production chain ('FairChain'). Moyee removes various middlemen from the chain and doesn't have the coffee beans roasted in a factory in the West, but in Ethiopia. The entire chain is up for discussion, a discussion that involves the consumer. This allows buyers to have an influence on a global problem without leaving their chairs: simply by buying a pack of coffee, they are acting simultaneously in the Netherlands, Ethiopia and the world. In the liquid world of the diopticon, you are both here and somewhere else, at the same time.

On the same continent, courageous entrepreneurs are inventing many new forms of banking that are no longer based on centralised thinking and long, bureaucratic chains and structures dating back to the era of paper ledgers. 'While many Western banks struggle with ancient IT systems and a top-heavy branch network, African banks may well have sounder foundations for the financial services of the future'[68] Examples include M-Pesa by Safaricom in Kenya, ubaA in Nigeria and Ecobank in Togo. In these cases, domains that used to be strictly separated are merging together: today, a mobile operator can be a bank – tomorrow, it could also be an insurer. Or a university.

Holacracy: the company as diopticon

Was Henry Ford such a great trail-blazer with his efficient car plant because he wanted to improve the working conditions of his employees? Not at all: the introduction of the production line on a grand scale allowed him to produce more with fewer workers. This in turn allowed Ford to innovate further, making the first car available to the middle class. In fact, his own workers could now join the middle class and buy their own Model T Fords.

Automation has gone way beyond the conveyor belt; robots have taken over most tasks in the factories. Instead of performing monotonous work in the factory, most workers want a challenge.

It's clearly time for something new: so why does our office work still look so much like Ford's industrial way of working, with its subtle coercion reminiscent of the panopticon? We still sit down at our desks from nine in the morning until five in the afternoon, when we can go home again. Like the job descriptions of the old Ford workers, our job descriptions today often leave little scope for creativity. And to make matters worse, some of us are physically put in a cubicle. Ford and his contemporary Taylor, who deconstructed the production process down to the smallest detail and made it more efficient, still dictate how we work.

A dioptical replacement for this worn out, rigid form of working is the holacracy, made popular by Brian Robertson who also drew up a constitution for this new system. Holacracy is a way of organising companies without traditional managers and job descriptions but based instead on overlapping, self-organising teams referred to in the jargon as circles. This concept elaborates on sociocracy, an alternative to democratic decision-making developed in the 1990s.

An organisation that functions in a holacratic way consists of 'circles' and 'cells' – the terminology reflects a belief in the organic functioning of organisations. These cells do not consist of people, but of roles that can be played by people. Most individuals play more than one role and are represented in various circles. This model doesn't so much do away with hierarchy altogether (you could still have 'higher' and 'lower' circles), but rather liquefies it.

Zappos, an online shoe retailer generating a turnover of a billion dollars and owned by Amazon, is the most striking example of a company that applies holacratic principles. The company ratified the *Holacracy Constitution* early in 2014, transferring the power of the CEO to the network. Tony Hsieh, who used to be the boss, is now the 'lead link' in the umbrella 'company wide circle' – although he retains the authority to have the decisive say in the event of an deadlock concerning the course to be taken. The company is doing well, because 'happy employees produce happy customers', as Hsieh says in every interview on the subject.

Although technology can be a good tool to help realise a holacracy (it takes quite a bit of coordination), according to its inventors this innovation is mainly social. It's all about how businesses can respond to a changeable, decentral reality and incorporate this into their internal structure. The result is a flexible organisation with self-managing teams that regularly revise their own assignments in the light of a changed context.

Not everyone believes in the holacratic model, however. It is sometimes seen as a plaything for enlightened despots who implement the concept in their organisation, only for it to evaporate the moment such an initiator leaves and be replaced again by a traditional, hierarchical organisation.[69] It also requires a great deal of consultation, and not everyone appreciates this ('just let me get on with my work!').

Everyone's a maker

It's being referred to as the 'industrial revolution of the twenty-first century': 3D printing, the computer-controlled production of physical objects.

The basic technology used in 3D printing is easy to understand. Using a computer model, a machine makes a physical object from one or more raw materials. The specific technologies can make use of polymers, metals, ceramics, paper, chocolate and countless other materials. The applications range from the production of parts for aircraft engines on site, which are lighter and more complex than if they are produced using other techniques, to downloading a design at home and printing out that one broken component for your coffee machine.

3D printing will, particularly in the longer term, have a huge impact on manufacturing. It is speeding up innovation because it is now possible to produce prototypes of new products much more quickly than in the traditional way. The time factor is still a challenge in relation to the end product –printing an object is often much slower than producing an object using traditional methods – but once again, Moore's law also applies to 3D printing: the technology is getting quicker and cheaper all the time.

The development of 3D printing goes hand-in-hand with advanced scanning and design technologies. Physical objects are becoming transparent – not because you can literally see through them, but because their internal architecture can be described in a file. Once such a file exists, anyone who can get their hands on the file can produce a copy of the object with the right printer and the right raw materials.

3D printing is leading to a significantly different economy, referred to by Peter Day of the BBC as the 'heartbeat economy.' According to him, the economy is shifting away from uniform products and services and more and more towards tailor-made products and an economy in which personal

service plays an ever-greater role and in which creative work
will replace repetitive work.

For many products, mass production will for a long time
continue to be a cheaper, quicker and more efficient means
of production than 3D printing, but in time this will be
overtaken by 3D printing for more and more applications.
The factory of the future will be in your home – decentralised
production holds great promise. The distinction between
private and commercial use will blur, as both will make use
of the same basic principles. This can be compared with
the rise of computer technology. At first, there was a huge
distance between the world of mind-bogglingly expensive,
room-filling mainframes for business and the world of hobby
computers for the pioneering amateur. Now, the two have
come together in the global cloud.

Perhaps the most revolutionary aspect of all is the merging of roles: now, the designer, maker and user can be one
and the same person. Due to the extremely short lines involved in the process, the traditional hierarchy and division
of labour have vanished from the production process. 3D
printing thus showcases an outstanding aspect of the diopticon: the merging of roles.

Merging roles

To sum up the insights about the diopticon: countless processes are moving towards decentralisation and transparency in a liquid structure in which it is possible to constantly
make and break connections. The boundaries between the
roles of citizen, employee and consumer are blurring: in
all three of these roles, people want to be in charge of their
own lives. This is the reality faced both by governments and
private organisations – innovative social and technological
possibilities can be seen as an external threat, or (much

better) as a tool for implementing change. The social fabric changes so rapidly that government bodies are have to rejuvenate themselves or become redundant; companies and non-profit organisations are facing the same challenges in a world no longer bound by national borders or the walls of the office building.

In short: from virtual currencies to businesses and political structures, the consequences for you and me are momentous. Our own roles are constantly changing because they are no longer embedded in a set pattern. New connections bring new value.

Both individuals and organisations therefore have to change at a relentless, almost revolutionary pace. As I stated earlier, we are changing from customers into 'prosumers'. From passive consumers, we begin to take part in the production process. We are generating our own power, on the roof or in the garden. Contributing some effort to interesting new products, we add the role of investor to that of the consumer, making us into 'consuvestors'. The old-fashioned banker and investor are left behind and the customer service department can be closed because the customer no longer exists. Angry neighbours are becoming police auxiliaries. A few years ago, an initiative called 'Burgernet' (the 'citizens' network') was set up in the Netherlands: the police send out descriptions of wanted people and vehicles by SMS. The million and a half Dutch citizens taking part have already helped solve numerous crimes, which is not only good for the general sense of justice, but also for the extent to which we can all participate in society. Of course, we will want something in return – no one is entirely without self-interest – so the police will at least have to tell us what they did with the information we provided. The vertical relationship with authority is changing into a horizontal one. From a rather paternalistic position, the police are taking on a more brotherly role – but hopefully not like Big Brother from *1984*.

The system, symbolised by the rules, regulations and institutions that affect our economic and social lives, sometimes
has trouble keeping up with these changes. An official permit for a taxi service in Amsterdam costs 11,880 Euros. I think
that's bizarre – why should I not be allowed to take someone
from A to B for a few Euros? My navigation software provides
the expertise that the taxi driver used to have a monopoly on.
No one needs this degree of controlling regulation aimed at
making sure we know our place as driver and customer, and
behave accordingly.

We have the possibility, and also the duty, to keep changing our own roles within society, in the midst of continuous
developments and an uncooperative system. (In Paris, Berlin
and Amsterdam, the rise of Uber caused taxi wars, exempli-
fying the stubbornness of the system.)

I deplore hard-headedness on the part of the system or individuals, although I am certainly not in favour of an unre-
stricted diopticon as described by Dave Eggers in *The Circle*.
If everyone and everything has become transparent, privacy
has disappeared completely and everyone is being driven
crazy by all the interaction, the diopticon has been taken too
far.

How can we ensure that the diopticon respects the human
scale? I believe that we need to look for new rules of play.

Making the diopticon workable

In a swimming pool, the rules are clear. Young children can
only go in the deep end with flotation devices. Inappropri-
ate touching is not allowed; nor is skinny dipping. There is a
lifeguard on duty. Sometimes you have to stay in your lane,
other times you can swim freely through the pool. If things
go wrong, you can be sure the rules will be tightened up.

At the risk of using a somewhat simplistic image, something similar can be observed in the liquid society. The pos-

THE DIOPTICON   105

sibilities it offers us may be circumscribed by rules we make
up and agree on as we go along. This allows us to prevent all
these possibilities leading to a horrific future that reduces
human life to the level of farce. We can make the diopticon
that suits us – on a human scale.

It will not be easy. Technological developments often
produce challenges that not the most creative science fiction
writer could have fathomed. To a certain extent, *The Circle*
already exists, but in a more subtle form, in such a way
that we don't even really know exactly how transparent we
actually are. This leads to uncertainty. In the meantime, the
powers that be use this uncertainty to try and steer developments in ways that suit them. Such opposing forces can
curtail the diopticon, but they can also have the opposite
effect. If every square metre of the city is now a hotel, for
example, it becomes ridiculous to impose fire safety regulations like we are used to. A desire to force the liquid society
into such old constraints can lead to new rigidity: the regulatory framework becomes much too dense, people no longer
understand it, enforcement is problematic, in short: the
possibilities opened up by the liquid society are not used to
the full.

The diopticon, with its merging roles, transparency and
decentralisation, constantly asks us: what do we want to
regulate, how can we do this effectively, and what do we let
go? The starting point should be that moving parts should
be able to move as freely as possible within certain limits.
Setting and monitoring these new limits will be one of the
major social challenges we will face in the decades ahead.

Both feet on the ground

A swimming pool has a bottom, and so does the liquid society. But now that I've arrived at the end of this chapter, I'll drop the metaphors for a moment to take a look at the various new bases that allow us, even in the midst of the diopticon, to keep both feet on the ground. A lot of these tools have existed for quite a while, although the speed of development sometimes forces us to use them for another purpose than the one they were designed for.

The sharing economy needs a sound base that requires that possession, property and access relate to one another in a new way. Insurance policies, regulatory frameworks and other components of the 'old' order must be rigorously examined in terms of their capacity to move with the times. In cases of doubt, rules should be abandoned – protection of the status quo may never be an aim in itself.

The basic income, once designed to protect those in the very lowest income bracket, could now offer protection to today's middle class. After all, it is the 'ordinary' jobs in the middle that are under most pressure. New assurances are needed so that freelancers and flexworkers can continue to thrive. The basic income can serve as a source of inspiration for such security. I will talk about work and income more in Chapter 6.

The various layers of government need to scratch their heads and have a good think. Will they become smart platforms, like Facebook and Amazon, or will the remain closed, solid 'black boxes'? Transparency is essential in at least two ways. Firstly, processes must be clear and transparent: for example, how to apply for a permit or how decisions are taken. Secondly, the technology used by the government must also be 'open'. Marleen Stikker, director of Amsterdam's Waag Society, puts forward an justified argument for the open city: all software used by the city must be 'open source' – if you add closed elements to this system, citizens can no longer form the networks they want to in the way they wish. In Chapter 7, I will look in greater depth at power, government and citizens' autonomy.

In education, we need to let go of rigid curricula; modern education should combine cognitive and individual development. Self-knowledge, the art of living and dealing with change are among the essential life skills of the citizen of the twenty-first century.

Lastly, in the next chapter I will elaborate – sorry! – on the swimming pool metaphor, under the title 'The Swimming Certificate'. It's just too apt a comparison: in the liquid society, we all have to learn to swim again. If we manage, the diopticon can land on its feet.

5

The Swimming Certificate

A proposal for a different approach to education and learning

In the last chapter, I described the diopticon – a model that helps us understand the liquid society. In order not to drown in this new reality, we will have to learn new skills. This makes education an important starting point, about which a lot it said, some of which makes sense and some doesn't. A few ideas stand out, such as Bildung and 'anti-disciplinary education'. Applied well, such ideas could equip us – and above all our children – with the skills they need to survive in changing times.

God, grant me the serenity to accept the things I cannot change,
The courage to change the things I can,
And the wisdom to know the difference.
Serenity Prayer by Reinhold Niebuhr

The house of ideals

It's a cliché: a drawing of the globe, with people of all different colours linking hands around the world. Making the world a better place – together, for everyone, and of course sustainably – is a natural desire. Walk into any primary school, look at the drawings and you will find one like this. The school is the house of ideals. The philosopher Peter Sloterdijk, who will appear again towards the end of this chapter, has his reservations: he sees a huge disconnect between the idealism of school and real life. He might be right, at least when the kind of idealism I encountered at my old primary school is involved, with its happy outlook on a malleable world that could and should be freed from racism and pollution of the environment. In the case of the primary school, this may be a good thing. It's alright for a twelve-year-old to have utopian ideas about the world and the possibility of changing it. After all, for kids and their parents, who look at their offspring's future from a perspective of malleability, life is all about hope.

The institution of education is an essential 'middleman' to whom parents entrust their children, a change machine aimed at turning naive young people, over time, into capable individuals. It categorises people, trains them on the basis of this categorisation and hands out certificates which – hopefully – will help them with the rest of their lives. This is done on the basis of all kinds of patterns and processes, many of which were developed decades or even centuries ago.

Around the school, society is changing: the knowledge you now gain at university will be obsolete in five years. The job that you are being trained for, won't exist in ten years' time. The iPad you learn to use at school will be hopelessly outdated by the time you graduatel.

Amidst all these changes, society raises the pressure on education. Since schools tend to be bureaucratic, conservative institutions, education reforms initiated by the government have the tendency to fail.

The Serenity Prayer quoted at the beginning of this chapter is applicable to education – besides serene patience, education demands a lot of courage. As I argued before, the middle of society is being transformed at a rapid pace, and education is in many ways right in the middle of the middle. I shall explain this in the next paragraph.

Education and the middle

Education is interesting in at least three ways in light of the idea that the middle has to reinvent itself:

1. Educators in the broader sense are traditional middlemen who mediate between people and their ideals (to stick with Peter Sloterdijk's terminology). This intermediary role is of great importance to society. This role should be changing as society changes, but that doesn't always work out.
2. People involved in education traditionally make up part of the middle class – the very middle class that is now under such pressure. I will discuss this further in the next chapter.
3. There is also a 'middle' inside schools: the middle managers (department managers, deputy heads, et cetera);

the ICT department; education support staff; in short all
the 'enablers' who are not actually teachers. In the case
of large educational establishments (often the result of
mergers and other forms of scaling up), there are many
additional intermediary layers involved with all kinds of
things except education itself.

In this chapter, I will deal with the changing role of education, and therefore also of the educator, embedded in the
question as to how we (and our children) should deal with
change. In doing so, I will focus largely on educators as middlemen. Nevertheless, my point on middle within the school
is also important, since I expect that the roles of teacher and
enabler will merge. The school of the future will be populated by coaches, mentors, didactics experts, professional specialists, technology experts and media specialists. Together,
they will help the children, young people and adults of the
future realise their ideals.

The merger of the roles of teacher and enabler does not
apply that everyone involved in education will have to be
an all-rounder. On the contrary. This, in fact, is one of the
problems with education as it is today, with teachers being
given the all but impossible task of catering almost entirely
independently to groups of between 25 and 30 young people.
They have to pass on knowledge, maintain order, provide
individual attention and keep up with the curriculum. If the
school walls were to be broken down (sometimes in a very
literal way), education professionals could perform better
because it would be easier for them to achieve the ideal mix
of tasks that does justice to their competences. I will return
to the ideal society and the ideal school below.

The certificate of change

As a child, I was a walking nightmare for my parents. Hyperactive, I'd rush around all over the place. I just couldn't be stopped. Water was a particular hazard: every water-filled ditch, river or pool exerted an irresistible attraction to me. I regularly fell into the water. My parents sent me off to swimming lessons the moment I was old enough. I got my swimming certificates at a very early age, so my parents could relax a little when we were out and about.

A swimming certificate is a clear-cut thing: you have to demonstrate a particular set of skills that mean you won't drown if you fall into the water. And even though it's many years since I got those certificates, I still have those skills.

In contrast, the skills and competences required for survival in the liquid society are different from those made of a hyperactive toddler by the water-filled ditch and the swimming pool. Because everything around us is changing so quickly, dealing with change has to be high on the list of things to learn. Certificates in this old sense seem rather outdated now, based as they are on a clearly defined package of skills and knowledge. You don't see 'Insight into Processes of Change' or 'Skills for Dealing with Change' on such certificates (yet).

It is possible to broaden this discussion further: organisations could also benefit from learning more about change. If ISO certificates for organisations can be compared with certificates presented to individuals, then the quality management certificate ISO 9001:2008 is a striking example. This certificate can be boiled down to 'say what you do, do what you say and prove it'. But there is as yet no reliable certification system for change management. There are six-day 'change management' courses, but these strike me as rather inadequate, to put it mildly. In Chapter 8, I will elaborate on how organisations should respond to change when managing talent, while letting go of rigid hierarchies.

The liquid society transforms individuals (and organisations) that were previously stratified in strict hierarchical relations into a bubbling tub of free radicals. More and more possibilities are opening up to establish new connections and to break them again. It will be interesting to see what people require to be able to engage in this process, and how that can be tested.

From maths tests to vision

Education is currently caught up in a race to the bottom. By focusing all our attention on those pupils lacking in ability and adjusting training and tests to suit them, society is failing to take the best pupils seriously, neglecting the group in between – and not helping the most vulnerable get much further.

A good example of this race to the bottom is the *No Child Left Behind* policy in the United States, in force until 2015. In a quest to make sure every young citizen meets a minimum level of literacy and math proficiency, the federal government imposed a system of rigourous testing. The accountability system that came with the policy punished states if not enough students scored too low on the many tests. Nation-wide criticism concerned both the role of federal government, a well as the culture of overtesting. With support from both the Democratic and Republican Parties, the legislation was replaced by the 'All Students Succeed Act', on which the U.S. Senate voted in December 2015.

The American politicians have been quite right in decentralising education. Futhermore, a culture of never-ending tests does not do justice to the uniqueness of every single individual young person. The politicians did miss a point, however: if the goal is leave *no* child behind to make *all* students succeed, education will still be a race to the bottom, the search for the very lowest level of acceptable mastery.

In my own country, a comparable situation exists. Early in 2015, the Dutch Cabinet proposed to make maths testing compulsory as part of the graduation in secondary education. The aim is to stimulate schools and pupils to brush up their poor arithmetic skills.

If you look up the test in question, you can't help noticing just how bad things must really be. It's hard to imagine how thousands of pupils could possibly fail to do these simply sums – some accompanied by a simple example and some not. Especially when you consider they get four tries at it.

There is nothing wrong with teaching pupils to do sums with a link to real life. The approach is problematic when it is part of a race to the bottom. That's alright for a company selling bargain-basement underwear, but for education, it's killing. The Dutch Cabinet wants this test to be 'part of the pass/fail equation': in other words, you have to pass the test to get your certificate. This focuses the discussion on the very lowest threshold we can set – which if necessary we have to drag pupils across by brute force to ensure they have a minimum proficiency in arithmetic. And then they get a certificate. It's a distorted discussion that doesn't do education any favours all at.

Fortunately, everyone agrees that education in general can do much better. The big question is how. A compulsory test can at best give a little stimulus, but does not automatically improve education. That takes vision. The debate should be about the future of education in a broader sense, and not about the political in-fighting around a specific measure imposed from above.

Possible solutions

Where should we look for solutions? What should a future certificate, for individuals and perhaps even for organisations, be about? I can think of a few pointers:

- Young people in particular switch increasingly quickly between information flows and learning through play. Today's children learn easily through gaming and are better able to multitask than previous generations. In this respect, Dutch Professor Wim Veen coined the phrase 'homo zappiens': a new type of person who learns much more flexibly and dynamically.
- Outside-of-the-box thinking – thinking outside of prescribed patterns and frameworks. This is needed to be able to stay on your feet in a rapidly changing society. 'Design-thinking' is a term often heard in this context-thinking in terms of experimentation and design – although the older ideal of *Bildung* is never far away in such discussions.
- There is a (literal) wall between classes being taught maths and classes being taught English, and this is often also the case with the various divisions within organisations too. Such compartmentalisation by discipline is out of date. Interdisciplinary thinking is not enough: the future belongs to the anti-disciplinary approach.
- 'Talentism' is a useful concept in relation to individuals, organisations and society. Individuals must be able to better get to know, develop and make use of their talents; organisations should set themselves up accordingly; it has been said concerning the broad organisation of society that 'talentism is the new capitalism'.
- Social capital acts like glue, holding the changing society together. People can join forces in many different ways to jointly take advantage of change.

- Besides knowledge transfer, education must take care of personal development, and prepare young people for successful preparation in society. In terms of the diopticon, this insight provides a concrete list of things to do: vary the size of the group, teach pupils to manage their time effectively and make sure attention is devoted to the art of living.

Let's explore some of these ideas in more detail.

Homo zappiens

I personally encountered this new type of person, 'homo zappiens', when in 2014 I was asked to support the annual opening of the Stenden Hogeschool in Leeuwarden, a professional university in the north of the Netherlands. The originator of the term 'homo zappiens' is Wim Veen, professor of education and technology at Delft University of Technology. In his book *Homo Zappiens. Growing up in a Digital Age* he explains the next generation of pupils, students, employees, citizens and consumers (you may read: prosumers). Like their parents, who zapped between TV channels, this new generation zap from e-mail to a game or chat, and then to their homework, or friends, or Skype.

The young homo zappiens can handle large quantities of information and quickly decide on its usefulness. They participate in various communities, online and offline, and don't differentiate between these. Teachers and parents must therefore wonder whether the climate these new people are growing up in is really suitable for them. The existing educational system was set up like one of Henry Ford's production lines. In groups of thirty, they cram for formal qualifications that are the same for everyone. And all this under the supervision of teachers who are expected to be superhuman: a repository of knowledge, an educator, a coach, a mentor and a role model, all at the same time. No teacher can do all of these things equally well, yet hardly any use is made of the possibilities for young people to teach themselves and one another. That is a shame: the education industry is leaving a huge source of value untapped. Why does our educational system cling to nineteenth-century ways of working?

Naturally, many people involved in education realise that the twenty-first century has dawned and pay lip-service to progress: dual-language education, personal profiles and iPads are promoted by many contemporary schools.

But an iPad for every pupil doesn't change much by itself: what's needed is a new mentality that corresponds to the changing minds of today's young people. The chancellor of the Radboud University thinks that all teachers teaching in pre-university education in the Netherlands should them-selves have a university degree. This is of course fine – there are certainly enough unemployed graduates out there – but it's hardly the point. Education has to change at a much more fundamental level. Why should you as a teacher try to explain a physics phenomenon when Stanford University has made a fantastic film on that very subject, available for free? Why ban telephones in the classroom if these do not distract pupils at all? Where is peer education? Solutions have to be tried out in practice, and we need to switch regu-larly to get the desired results. Just ask the homo zappiens.

Digital natives

The 'digital native' is young and (has already for a long time been) oriented towards the digital: many people have expressed the opinion that s/he is the bringer of change par excellence. In much of the literature on young people (which often typifies generations by using a letter: generation Y, generation Z), it is assumed that thanks to their technical know-how young people are better able to use technology than older people, from a very early age. I would like to express the caveat here that being able to use technology well doesn't happen by itself – undesirable behaviour such as online bullying and scandals involving the dissemination of explicit photos speak volumes in this context. Howeveras long as there is support and supervision, early exposure to a new system of logic can benefit the young mind in the longer term. Compare this to the way we learn language: research on learning a second language has clearly shown that if you start learning a new language at an early age, the learning process later in life will also be quicker.

Worldwide, interesting developments are taking place concerning the digital native. In South Korea, 99.6 percent of children are categorised as digital natives – in the Netherlands it's 98.4 percent. With 95.6 percent, the United States is lagging behind somewhat, while in Russia 49.6 percent of children fall into this category. In Iraq, the figure is just 2.5 percent. Worldwide, digital natives are in the minority, although their numbers are expected to double between 2013 and 2018.

Figure 5.1

Learning to think differently

Technology is not an aim in itself and inspirational, effective change is not all about gadgets. I believe education benefits from young people being caused to think in different ways (making use of technology, of course). Relevant terms in this respect range from outside-of-the-box thinking to *Bildung*. What exactly does that entail?

Outside-of-the-box thinking refers to independent thought for original solutions. The puzzle shown in Figure 5.1 is a nice example. Try to join the nine dots together by drawing four continuous lines. Give it a go. (You can find the solution on the next page in Figure 5.2.)

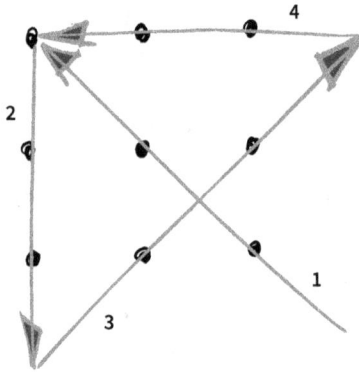

Figure 5.2

Thinking outside of the established frameworks every now and again is literally and figuratively a good idea. Particularly in formal education (education provided by a recognised institution that prepares people for the world of work and life in general by issuing certificates), there are quite a few such frameworks: study goals, standards, requirements. It is a challenge to break free from these rigid constraints.

Bildung

A word that crops up in this context is *Bildung*, usually used to refer to 'inner development' or 'general development.'

It is supposed to contribute to pupils' ability to place their own concrete knowledge and skills in the right perspective. The term was used by the German linguist, philosopher and statesman Wilhelm von Humboldt (1767-1835) and is usually not translated. According to Humboldt, knowledge, morality, judgement and critical thought go hand in hand, and Bildung equips the young to face the future. In the conceptual framework of this German academic, *Bildung* is opposed to *Ausbildung*, which refers to specialist (academic) training or learning.

Such thorough and multifaceted general development is not for everyone; there is an aristocratic quality to Humboldt's thought, which is perhaps not so strange given the age of the term.

All manner of recent pleas for 'Bildung' in education underline the term's currency, as a counterweight to a society which, through its educational system and economy, likes to categorise us.

Such discussions are all the more crucial as, in spite of a periodical round of reforms, we still organise our educational system as if the industrial revolution had just taken place. Labels rule and young people roll off the conveyor belt in groups of thirty, stamped with a standardised grade. Pupils are divided up into equal groups and the day is divided up into equal blocks of time in which a specialist instructs them in their specialist subject. This is how it has been since the nineteenth century, and you and I grew up with it. In a dynamic society, however, in which the competences for success shift every five years, this is simply not good enough.

Sloterdijk is pessimistic: he doesn't believe the ideal of *Bildung* can be implemented in a realistic way within our current educational system, which is not geared to satisfying existential curiosity and sniffing out generally accepted norms and general knowledge, but is geared instead to 'the management of disillusionment.'[70] The state doesn't like dreamers and forces the education system into 'the production of cognitive people in the service of the world of work and power politics.'[71]

Sloterdijk has a point, also in relation to the situation in the Netherlands. Here, innovation and variation make their way into education only with great difficulty. The political establishment in The Hague calls the shots, and this can lead to a top-down approach with blunt instruments. Standards too low? Then certification of teachers and a minimum of 1,040 hours of classroom teaching a year are imposed from above. Problems with arithmetic and language? Then just abolish the cultural and social subjects and get back to teaching sums and learning words, and then measure the results and test, test, test! Teachers, worn out by all the changes and imposed measures, try to do what they have always done in a new way following the latest change of course – and end up more and more frustrated.

First Bildung, then practice

The book *One Size Does Not Fit All: A Student's Assessment of School* was written by seventeen-year-old New York pupil and entrepreneur Nikhil Goyal[72]. This young high-flyer probes how schools deal with one of the most valuable raw materials virtually all young people possess: creativity. 'Schools can't just introduce a "creativity hour" and that's that,' he writes. He argues that the subjects English, mathematics and history should be dropped. Instead, he proposes that the syllabus be focused around big ideas, issues and conundrums: big life puzzles.

I find this an interesting thought process. It goes further than the ideal expressed by *Bildung*, which argues for scope for general development alongside concrete *Ausbildung* (training). Perhaps, particularly in the liquid society, it would be a good idea to turn the whole thing around: first the big life puzzles, which naturally present to learners the obstacles they then have to surmount (with the requisite support). In this vision, practical skills such as arithmetic and language are subordinate to achieving the goal: learning to solve the problems life throws at you.

If you set up schools in line with this idea, there is still employment for professionals who are skilled in introducing young people to language and sums; it's just no longer a matter of course that these will be part of subjects such as language and arithmetic or English and maths, each taught in 50 minute time slots, with a written test next week.

Anti-disciplinary education

Goyal is in favour of 'anti-disciplinary education', a term adopted from Sandy Pentland of the Media Lab, and in which we are all malleable, literate system-oriented thinkers capable of solving problems, posing questions and analysing a subject. This would bring education into the twenty-first century and transform young people into inspired agents of change equipped with the appropriate skills and tools. School-leaving exams and national curricula can then be abandoned wherever possible.

Goyal condemns America's *No Child Left Behind* policy, and the same argument applies to the discussion about a compulsory arithmetic test in the Netherlands: these represent a one-sided fascination with the lowest acceptable level or reading and arithmetic and a failure to recognise the potential of good education aimed at stimulating young people's natural curiosity. Instead of this, young people are asked to jump through hoops to achieve good scores in standardised tests of dubious merit. Goyal argues for a system of education with school leaving qualifications as open as possible in order to allow schools the greatest possible freedom to find an appropriate way to stimulate children's curiosity.

As an example, he cites Finland, where this is already happening.

The traditional, common model Goyal so loathes corresponds exactly to the panopticon I described in Chapter 4: the pupil is an object and the teacher the untouchable watchman at the centre. Education could look very different in a diopticon. The partitions between subjects would be broken down; pupils would constantly make connections (and break them again); hierarchies and division of tasks among teachers would largely disappear; standardised tests would be redundant. This would require schools to be literally redesigned: if pupils themselves are allowed to go in search of answers, it is logical to work sometimes in small groups or individually and at other times in a larger group. If a particular teacher is a great speaker, why not let them address a hundred people at once, and record it to enable future pupils to watch it later?

Design thinking

The idea to subordinate educational disciplines to a higher goal resounds with an interesting new perspective that is gaining ground: design thinking. I first came across this when I was involved in an interesting project concerning the merger of two universities of applied sciences in Leeuwarden. Design thinking was to be the educational concept underlying the new, merged universities. After speaking to many students, administrators and teaching staff, I became enthusiastic about this new approach.

Design thinking turns education (and other processes) upside down. It places the person (rather than the process) at the centre, is based on cooperation (rather than hierarchy) and is experimental (instead of tested and calibrated). In the same way a designer makes a sketch or builds a prototype which can still change in very many ways, with design thinking the educator puts a pupil or student to work, sending them in search of a challenge and instructing them to solve this by experimentation. Instead of a rigid curriculum with subjects imposed upon the student, the student asks for the knowledge, skills and tools she or he needs. Instead of cramming for final examinations, challengers are formulated, and instead of ticking off a list of subjects, students build up a portfolio.

Although design thinking can certainly claim to be a very modern trend, it certainly doesn't focus on tricks and gadgets: the design mentality is not something – like an iPad – you can just bring into the classroom in the hope it will improve education. It is a change of mentality that can prepare people for the future.

Université 42

While in the USA high school students still stress about their test scores, and pupils in technical, higher or pre-university secondary schools in the Netherlands cram for their final exams, an innovator in Paris has totally redesigned education, including elements from design-thinking and the anti-disciplinary approach of Nikhil Goyal. This new education is called Université 42, a private school on software development.

What is the answer to life, the universe and everything? Any nerd can tell you, as can Google. Or read the novel I referred to above, *The Hitchhiker's Guide to the Galaxy* by Douglas Adams, and you will find out that wealthy Parisian übernerd Xavier Niel (founder of and major shareholder in French internet giant Free) named his new programming course after the inimitable answer to that impossible question. The Université 42 offers an open learning environment and passionate collaborative projects in which students evaluates one another's work. The school is open 24 hours a day, 365 days a year. The entrance requirement is ambition – no certificates are required. Applications for the first year amounted to staggering numbers. The selection process is called (how appropriately for this book) The Swimming Pool and filters out the best one thousand from four thousand applicants.

Université 42, as a private educational institute, is very sure of its role: demand for coders will not be diminishing any time soon.

It is highly instructive that it is in private education, not subject to the limitations of regulation and state financing, where education is being organised in a completely new way. The everyday practice of state-financed education is more recalcitrant – not only because of the levels of finance involved, but also because of the government's tendency to tie everything up in rules and regulations. It is quite difficult to organise schooling in varying group sizes, crossing boundaries between disciplines and ages, since government-imposed requirements are based on these well-tested and objectifiable indicators. All quality standards applied by the school inspection are based on teaching in the classroom.

Université 42 is proof of the argument that it is sometimes possible to formulate answers even though you do not yet know the right question. This is exactly the challenge education is facing: we cannot be at all sure what the future will demand of young people, but one thing is for sure: we should try to prepare them for it. In the next chapter, I will quote a witty list of future top jobs, including 'avatar manager' and 'time broker'. What such jobs will actually be like in practice, no one yet knows.

The point is that we do not need to know, if only education teaches young people to keep learning throughout their lives and not to obsess about final exams. Education can best deal with the changes taking place in society by itself being innovative. Not in a regimented way, but by providing a rich and varied range of choices for a rich and diverse world; for a future employment market we know little about and, most important of all, through which young people can discover their own qualities.

Taming time

I stated above that the liquid society's relationship to time, with technological development as a 'steady drumbeat in the background', is different from that of its predecessor. Change as a constant power that accelerates change is a difficult factor to deal with in education. The skills you learn today may be redundant in five years' time. How to deal with this? The answer from the current education establishment is pretty clear: just don't. In the education of the future, a start could be made by defining the concept of 'time' in a more liquid way than at present: less rigid timetabling, less time spent 'penned up' in the classroom and more time for pupils and students to spend autonomously on projects and subjects they feel passionately about. In this context, 'autonomously' certainly does not mean 'freely': young people in particular need good mentoring on how to spend their time. Setting goals, working towards these and increasing efficiency do not come naturally to those undergoing puberty. The current answer to this developmental stage is a rigid system of planning imposed from above; an alternative could be time-management training. My assignment for the new type of school would be to teach pupils to set ambitious goals, but also to teach them to adjust these goals in line with their advancing insights. This can only be done if education is tailor-made. All young people enter school as different and unique individuals, and they all should be equally different when they leave.

A new certificate

In this chapter, I have extensively talked about schools in relation to the society these schools are preparing pupils for. I see a renewed focus on *Bildung* as a challenge to society (and education in the first place) to organise itself not in a top-down but a bottom-up manner which generates social capital, focuses on the development of individual talent and the major challenge of learning to function in a rapidly changing, connected world. What would the new certificate, suitable for digital natives, be like in such a world?

I can sum up this chapter in the ten properties of the swimming certificate for the liquid society:

1. The certificate itself is malleable: it is a never-ending story undergoing continuous development.
2. Change is not only a characteristic of the certificate itself, but also an important subject covered by the certificate: your ability to think outside-of-the-box about new problems and to continue to develop new skills is far more important than your knowledge and skills at this present moment.
3. The certificate is specific to you: what counts is the individual human being. As a homo sapiens, you have individual rights and you are (hopefully) able to make life decisions for yourself. You have learned things you didn't know or couldn't do before within the choices you have made and the talents you possess, and these set you apart from others.
4. This knowledge and ability can usually only really be useful within a group context. You can therefore score points for your personal contribution to the social capital of the group. In other words, you are rewarded for your ability to cooperate, feel empathy, help others and to listen.

5. The certificate is a guarantee that its holder can ask questions (answering them is less important) and has a focus on the ability to learn. Technology can lend a helping hand.
6. There's not much point having a certificate if it doesn't have any effect on how others see you. Therefore, peer evaluation is part of the certificate, so you will need to build yourself a reputation..
7. Self-examination is a crucial skill and activity, and the certificate should reflect this.
8. The certificate exists within the context of the changing society. Whatever you do with your life, whatever career you choose, your environment will always be the political, social and economic reality.
9. The certificate does not entail central examinations, compulsory testing or standardised school leaving qualifications.
10. Disclaimer: this certificate is a thought exercise and not an actual certificate – but it can't hurt to compare existing certificates to it and, where necessary, bring these more into line with current (and future) requirements.

What we in practice call a certificate has characteristics that are very different from the virtual (not yet existing) swimming certificate for the liquid society. In everyday practice, it is a piece of paper which seems designed principally as a ticket into the employment market. This market – like the rest of society – is changing at an incredible pace. To what extent, I will discuss in the next chapter.

6

Work and value

What the end of the middle entails for employees and entrepreneurs

In the previous chapters, I discussed innovation, introduced the diopticon as a new model for the liquid society and spoke out in a plea for modern education. In this chapter, I will elaborate on the addition of value. After all, one of the 'middles' that is disappearing from society is the middle class. I will try to find out whether work will survive (the answer will be 'yes', but not without a 'but'). Work and value are undergoing some radical change.

Everything of value is defenceless
enriched by touchability
equal to everything
like the heart of time
like the heart of time
Lucebert[73]

New functions

In Douglas Adams' novel *The Hitchhiker's Guide to the Galaxy*, the main character finds himself inside a gigantic space ship. He comes across hundreds of sarcophagi with names and professions on them: TV producers, insurance agents, hairdressers, personnel managers, telephone cleaners, creative directors, PR consultants and management consultants. It turns out these are the useless professions of the planet Golgafrincham, sent into space on a pretext by the rest of the Golgafrinchans who actually do contribute something useful to society. Douglas Adams holds up a revealing mirror to us through these redundant citizens of a planet far, far away. It is worth wondering whether the jobs we do today will still be relevant in the future. The profile of the useless made me think of another list: a witty summing up by Jessica Winch in *The Telegraph* of the jobs which in the future might be very lucrative. A selection:

1. *Wellness consultant. Offers personal, holistic care for the elderly.*
2. *Body-part maker. Creates new limbs and other body parts for athletes and soldiers.*
3. *Nano-medic. Creates very small implants for health monitoring and self-medication.*

4. *Vertical farmer: Farms crops upwards rather than across flat fields to save space.*
5. *Avatar manager: Designs and manages holograms of virtual characters.*
6. *Memory augmentation surgeon: Helps preserve and improve memory in an ageing population.*
7. *Time broker: Handles time banked by customers in lieu of money for goods or services.*
8. *Personal branding manager: Develops and manages your personal brand.*
9. *Child designer: Designs offspring that fits parental requirements.*[74]

It is an entertaining list of future professions. Some of these jobs respond to future technologies, others emphasize the growing demand for care in an ageing population, some are a bit of both. The list does jump to conclusions: automation will of course continue and we will all live to be older, but there is no way of knowing what exactly the jobs of the future will be like and how many people will find work in them.

Middle class and middle income

The present reality is that the middle incomes are under immense pressure. Dutch-American sociologist Saskia Sassen discusses this problem in her book *Expulsions*. According to Sassen, 65 percent of jobs lost in 2008 were middle-class jobs. Of the new jobs created since then, just 25 percent are in the middle class.[75]

In her book, Sassen goes further. She argues that we are being forced out: out of the employment market, out of places to live, even out of the biosphere that makes life possible. In her view, financial-economic relations have become complex and brutal, resulting in massive inequality and dying nature. The usual terms 'poverty' and 'injustice' are no longer adequate; Sassen suggests that the word 'expulsion' is more applicable. The economy, of which the financial world is an ever more important part, is expelling original inhabitants from their surroundings, hard workers from their jobs and even the unemployed from the statistics: 'There comes a point when the long-term unemployed disappear from the radar – not because they have found work, but because they no longer sign on. They become invisible.'[76]

There is no clear-cut definition of the middle class. In discussions on the rise of the middle class in Africa, experts often refer to people who are no longer among the very poorest. Thus, people with at least 2 or 10 dollars a day to spend are counted among the middle class, depending who is reporting.

When we talk about middle incomes, we often talk about the relative share of the group in the middle as compared to the rest. What we are really discussing, then, is the distribution of income. This can be analysed using the Gini coefficient, a good tool for mapping income differences between people (or countries). The Gini coefficient is zero in the case of perfect income equality and 1 in the case of maximum inequality.

Figure 6.1 shows the Gini coefficients for Western countries. It shows –as you would expect – that inequality is greatest in the USA and that income differences are smallest in Scandinavia.

Thus, the distribution of income is most skewed in the USA. For many decades, America had the richest, biggest middle class, but that honour now goes to Europe. During the past three decades, both the lower and middle sectors in Europe have progressed more than in the United States.[77] The share of working people earning between 75 and 125 percent of the median income (the commonly used standard for looking at middle incomes) is almost 50 percent in

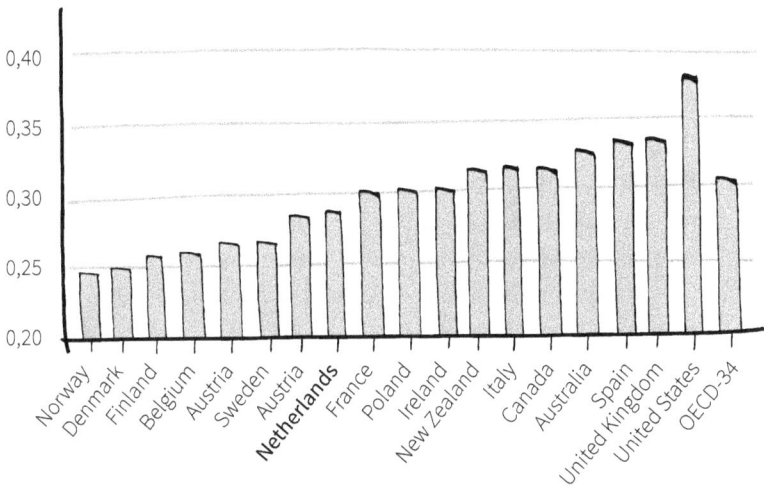

Figure 6.1

Scandinavia, but not even one third in the United States. In twelve countries within Europe (including Germany, Poland and Belgium) this number has fallen during the past twenty years.[78]

Even in the traditional middle-class bastion of France, citizenry, politics and press sound the alarm. A good example of the malaise is the situation on the housing market. Some ten million French people are experiencing difficulty finding a suitable home close to work. People who work in Paris and enjoy a middle-class income sometimes have to travel 60 or 70 kilometres just to get to work. There may be some cheap small hotels in the central arrondissements of the French capital, but don't even try to find affordable permanent housing in those neighbourhoods.

When thinking about the middle of the employment market, we don't think only about income, but also about the level of education. Exactly the same trend can be seen in Europe. In every EU country, the number of jobs at this level has declined since the year 2000. According to the statistics,

20 percent of employment in this segment has disappeared – while both the upper and lower levels have grown a little.[79]

Explanations for the disappearance of the middle

There are various explanations for the erosion of middle incomes. The American academic Marianne Cooper discusses a number of characteristics of neo-liberal economic relations. She refers to the impact of globalisation, the weakened role of labour unions and the neoliberal shift of risk towards the individual.[80] In addition, she points to the rise of the services sector: a development completely unrelated to the political colour of our current economic policy. 'While the manufacturing sector tends to create good jobs at every employment level, the service sector tends to create a relatively small number of high-skill, high-paying jobs (in fields like finance, consulting, and medicine) along with a large number of low-skill, low-paid jobs (in retailing, child care, and hospitality). The result is that secure, semiskilled middle-income jobs like those that once fuelled the rapid expansion of the American middle class are increasingly hard to find.'[81]

She makes an interesting point here: it is exactly these creative, innovative jobs, found on Jessica Winch's list, of which there will be a great shortage. This presents both a risk and an opportunity. The risk is that society will be educating people for a category of dwindling jobs. The opportunity is that, with the right mix of man and machine, we will have employment for most people with a healthy dose of self-knowledge.

We can safely say that there will not be huge numbers of jobs for specialists such as child designers and nano-medics. But wellness consultants – a creative, extremely human occupation – we can justifiably hope there will be room for many of these in our ageing society. Here too, there is a caveat: by the time it will be possible to earn your living with this type of job, technology will be so far advanced that a single wellness consultant can perhaps serve hundreds of clients, which is good for affordability, but not for employment.

Frans Blom of The Boston Consultancy Group puts it like this: 'If we extrapolate this trend as far as it will go, there will be two types of employees left over. Those who can keep up with the international march of civilisation and win a place in international value chains thanks to their high-value knowledge of new technology, for example app developers, PR professionals or engineers specialised in high-value infrastructure. Then there will be people offering local (non-market) services which, for the time being at least, are not subject to international competition or technological development: hairdressers, nurses or contruction workers, for example.'[82] Employment will still be found at the ends of the spectrum, but in the middle it will dwindle. People in the middle segment with a good education will then have little choice but to take jobs requiring less education at a lower scale in the employment market ladder: people with vocational training will be stacking shelves.

People often blame the technology itself for this. You will often hear the complaint, 'computers are taking our jobs!' It's time to get the robots discussed in Chapter 3 out.

Technological unemployment

In *The Second Machine Age* referred to in chapter 2, McAfee and Brynjolffson carry out a thought experiment called 'the android experiment.'[83] Imagine a company came up with a robot that can do everything a human being can do. Imagine that there is an endless supply of these robots and they cost virtually nothing to purchase and maintain. The consequences would be enormous: no one would work anymore because the robots would take over all the work without complaint. In other words, everyone will lose their jobs. There will however be entrepreneurs who continue to come up with new products and services that are developed extremely quickly at a low cost and delivered or facilitated by robots. In the old days, people with no property could still work, but because their work has now lost its value, they will be permanently stuck at home. For the people who own robots, this new world will be a land of milk and honey. For those without any property to speak of, it will mean grinding poverty.

McAfee and Brynjolfsson use this imaginary scenario to illustrate their fear of 'technological unemployment': the unemployment arising because of jobs disappearing owing to technological development. This term was first used in 1930 by the economist John Maynard Keynes, who identified the problem but saw it as a temporary 'maladjustment'. In the long run, Keynes believed, humankind will solve this economic asymmetry: 'I would predict that the standard of living in progressive countries one hundred years hence will be between four and eight times as high as it is to-day.'

Keynes was a prescient thinker: the forecast progress in both technology and standard of living did in fact come about after World War II, without mass unemployment. Many economists still believe that technology in a form Keynes could not have predicted will eventually lead to economic growth. In this respect, the Jevons paradox (named after William Stanley Jevons, who lived in the late nineteenth century) is relevant. Jevons described how greater efficiency in the use of a raw material (in Jevons' time, coal)[84] brought down the price of energy, but also created greater demand and thereby economic progress. This is a paradox because, at first sight, you would expect increased efficiency of energy use to lead to a decrease in the amounts used. The industrial revolution is proof of the contrary.

In the case of robots, you could argue that mankind 'will think of something new' if these machines take over all kinds of jobs from us. We can take up poetry, become an educational technology expert or work with children. A new balance could be found with a bigger cake to share and thus, on average, we will be richer. This will of course take a while.

McAfee and Brynjolfsson comment as follows on the subject: 'Once one concedes that it takes time for workers and organisations to adjust to technical change, then it becomes apparent that accelerating technical change can lead to widening gaps and increasing possibilities for technological unemployment. Faster technological progress may ultimately bring greater wealth and longer lifespans, but it also requires faster adjustments by both people and institutions. With apologies to Keynes, in the long run we may not be dead, but we will still need jobs.'[85]

The robots are stealing our jobs

How quickly this technological change will happen is shown in an interesting report by Oxford University in which researchers Frey and Osborne conclude that there is a good chance that no less than 47 percent of jobs in the United States will have been automated within twenty years.[86] The media have picked the message up, producing one-liners along the lines of: 'in twenty years robots will have taken half of all jobs.' But reality is a little more complex than that. Apart from the fact that the research was limited in scope – for example, it only deals with the USA – its conclusions give some grounds for optimism, even in America. Firstly, it is reassuring that, according to the researchers, the majority of jobs are only at a low risk of being made redundant by automation, in spite of the rapid development of technology. And it might be the case that there will be sufficient opportunities for the 'losers' to do other things which are made possible by technology – this was not covered by the research. One thing is for sure: technological innovation causes the labour

market to continue to to change extremely rapidly and automation will become a major factor in many areas.

Innovation has always had a huge effect on jobs. Let
me give you a brief historical overview. In the nineteenth
century, technology took over a lot of work from trained
craftsmen, replacing it with unskilled labour. Jobs that used
to be carried out by a single craftsman were broken down
into smaller tasks that could be performed by people with a
lower level of skill. Ford's conveyor belt is the most efficient
example: every worker has a very limited job, meaning the
total pressure of work is reduced by a few dozen percent in
relation to the much more highly trained (and much more
expensive) craftsman. The arrival of electricity in the early
twentieth century made even more people redundant. The
increased demand for relatively better trained blue collar
workers to operate the increasingly complex machines
forced those with less training to seek employment in the
emerging services sector. The level of education and training
shot up, as a result of which many workers were now able
to perform more complex, mental work. Also, the wages for
workers with a much higher level of training in the white
collar segment were not that much higher than those of their
blue-collar counterparts in the factories. The middle classe
emerged and became a regular feature of society. The age of
individualism arrived; in the USA, suburb after suburb was
built and in Europe the churches emptied out.

This is followed by the computer revolution, making many
of the jobs the middle classes had taken on much easier.
What is the result of this on the employment market? Some
argue that technology is a threat to all kinds of jobs at all
levels – but Maarten Goos and Alan Manning of the London
School of Economics disagree. In 2003, they introduced the
term 'job polarisation': in a relative sense, the jobs in the
middle are disappearing while 'lovely jobs' in the higher
segment and 'lousy jobs' in the lower remain. Their explana-

tion for this is as follows: the middle class does jobs that are difficult for a person but not for a machine (like bookkeeping, for example), while the lowest paid jobs are a piece of cake for a person but very difficult for a robot (like flipping hamburgers). There is a nice little film made about ten years ago which shows a robot cleaning up a child's room – the makers subsequently admitted they had operated the robot by remote control. Robot nannies are not yet on the horizon. In the meantime, wages in the top segment are rising, as the same automation is ensuring that these people can do their jobs more efficiently, while computers are not yet capable of producing their unique contribution (creativity, insight, strategy). This erosion of the middle can be represented on a U-shaped graph, with the relative number of jobs in the middle decreasing while the jobs to the left and right increase. This development can be seen in the USA, Europe and other developed countries. A direct consequence of this – and one which can already be seen in practice – is ever greater income inequality. Families are being hit particularly hard by this.[87]

The European image is painted in the graphs in figure 6.2. In the UK, the Netherlands and the EU, the occupations with an intermediate level of pay have declined in comparison to the low and high segments in the period between 1993 and 2010[88].

The middle class, at one time the great emancipator of entire generations, is in danger of perishing in the heat of the economic battle. There is enough simple, low-paid work and the people at the top aren't shy about accepting big rewards for their efforts. It's the 'man in the street' who, caught in the middle, may los out. Perhaps it would be useful to take a look at exactly which jobs we are talking about and the precise effect of technology on them.

Frey and Osborne, referred to above, use a quantitative approach to try to indicate which jobs are at risk of being

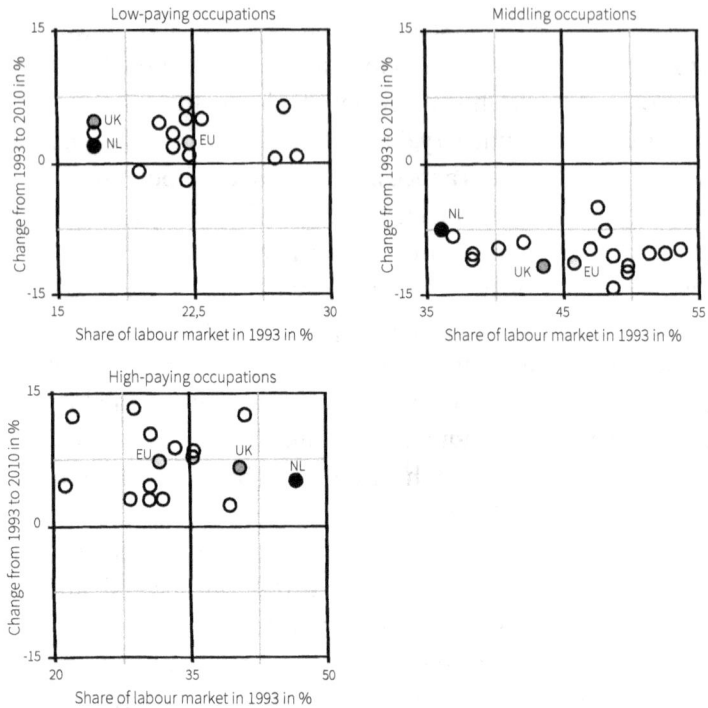

Figure 6.2

taken over by technology during the next 'twenty years or
so.' To do this, they looked at 702 jobs and assessed to what
extent these were impacted by three obstacles to automation: perception and manipulation, creative intelligence and
social intelligence. It is by no means just routine, easy jobs
that robots can now take over: the researchers correctly state
that the ability of computers to recognise complex patterns is
increasing. A good example is the self-driving car. As recently
as 2004, scientists were arguing that making a left turn (or
right in countries that drive on the left) posed so many problems because of approaching traffic, that it would be difficult
to imagine how the behaviour of a driver in such a situation could be copied. Apparently it wasn't so difficult after

all. Less than ten years later, the first self-driving car drove through the streets of Los Angeles. Now, computers are easily able to find their way around, given the right information. Two major factors in this are processing power and big data. Both are still increasing in accordance with Moore's law, so the time when a self-driving car rolls along your street is probably closer than you think.

The lower down the ladder, the more expendable

Frey and Osborne see an inverse proportionality between the 'class' of a job and the ease with which it can be replaced. They say: the lower the pay and the educational level required, the higher the chance that robots could take over a job. According to this theory, the lowest category will be hit harder than the middle category. I have my doubts about this, and will give three possible reasons why the future of the middle will, to put it mildly, be challenging.

Firstly, there will be political and social pressure to keep people employed. This will logically happen not so much in the middle but at the lower end of the market – for example, all those freelancers scrabbling around to earn a crust. These jobs are not highly valued.

Secondly, far-reaching automation means that the top is less and less dependent on the middle. The very highest level can make clever use of computer science to work more efficiently, making higher middle roles redundant. This development no longer impacts just the secretary, who has already lost the typing and archivist roles – more highly qualified work starts to disappear as well. For example, the legal researcher is under pressure because lawyers, armed with smart computer systems that can select applicable jurisprudence and even prepare draft texts, can work extremely dynamically and efficiently without a hoard of helpers.

Thirdly: jobs are usually not made up of just one single task, but a package of tasks – and this applies in particular to the jobs in the middle. The rise of dynamic platforms is interesting in this respect. These allow work to be organised in a much less hierarchical manner as, with the help of technology, each project can be organised and paid for differently, without the need for bureaucracy and management layers. So it could be that a specialist who is best at a particular part of a task is more attractive to clients than a generalist operating as a jack-of-all-trades.

A sixth robot

According to the accepted wisdom, computers develop the ability to replicate human tasks as well as possible using processing power and big data. Frey and Osborne also seem to subscribe to this view. The self-driving cars in California indeed do exactly this. The route is extensively reconnoitred and all the data is saved in the cloud. In other words, a set of rules is developed with which the computer has come quite close to what a human can do in this specific context.

Humans, however, learn to apply this skill in very different environments. While computers make adjustments only on the surface, the human brain constantly reinvents itself when learning. Computers may catch up with humans in this respect, which brings us to the sixth type of robot I discussed in Chapter 4. I referred to IBM's TrueNorth project which is all about making computer technology work more like the neural networks in the human brain. The human race and the employment market will face a whole new situation if and when computers are no longer hard-wired but become able to re-programme themselves. Such a new computer may have capabilities that make jobs redundant at all levels.

Man and robot side by side

A cyborg is a man-machine: ranging from assimilated biological beings in a high-tech beehive (like the Borg from *Star Trek*) to Darth Vader (from *Star Wars*). These organic computers are featured extensively in popular culture and literature, usually in a frightening incarnation. Their super-human powers are great for thrillers or even horror films, taking advantage of our human fear of technology.

The amalgamation of man and computer is now taking on very concrete but more innocent forms. You can wear an iWatch to tell the time, and it also measures your heartbeat. A pacemaker makes sure your heart keeps beating in the right way. In the not too distant future, nano-bots could well be circulating through your veins, regulating your vital functions.

Such robots appeared in Chapter 2 as the fifth type of robot, an combination of the strengths of human and machine, which in some tasks functions better than just a computer or just a human. The example I gave there was the freestyle chess tournament in which teams compete against one another without restrictions; it turns out the combination of good human chess players and good algorithms beats teams made up of just brilliant chess players or just the best algorithms.

More proof that man and algorithm work well together came in 2014 from the company Deep Knowledge Ventures, a venture capital company working in the pharmaceutical sector. This company appointed an algorithm called Vital to its Management Board and allows this algorithm to actually vote on investment decisions.[89] Of course, the fact that the algorithm 'votes' is a gimmick; in practice, the algorithm comes up with a recommendation and the human members of the Board take this into account in the decision-making process. This does however underline that decision-makers in the commercial sector can no longer do without the intelligence provided by machines.

PayPal also has good experiences with the man/machine combination. PayPal initially developed software to detect and block fraudulent transactions in a fully automated way, but it turned out that thieves were able to counter this strategy too quickly. The company's director, Peter Thiel, therefore decided on a hybrid approach: 'Human analysts [...] were not easily fooled by criminals' adaptive strategies. So we rewrote the software to take a hybrid approach: the computer would flag the most suspicious transactions, and human operators would make the final judgment.' This 'man-machine' symbiosis kept PayPal afloat. 'Fascinated by automation, most people still overlook the role that humans play in running software that would be worthless on its own.'

Interfaces

Cooperation between man and machine is also taking on other forms. Where man and machine are not yet seamlessly merging, interfaces are needed. A handy operating system on a mobile phone makes a cyborg's life a lot easier, for example. The simpler the interface, the more value people can get from their machine. Jaron Lanier, mentioned above, believes that the economy will increasingly revolve around machines that mediate in human social behaviour, much more so than the political system or policies do at present. This will transform the economy into a large-scale, systemic version of the design of user interfaces. 'Making complexity easier is the great craft of our era,' Lanier says.[90]

There are considerable opportunities for interesting work to make this happen. For example, a great number of people is needed to precisely gear the interfaces of apps, operating systems, games and other software to users' needs. This could even lead to technological innovation putting more

people to work and helping to reduce income inequality.
It won't be long before we can operate computers with our
voices, bringing ever more complex actions within the reach
of employees with a relatively low level of training. A computer that could deal with the following instruction would be
very useful indeed: 'Find the cheapest wholesale suppliers of
this screw.' A pretty complicated task at present, for which at
the moment the poor carpenter has to spend a while sitting
at his laptop. Flexible, tailor-made help from computers
would work wonders, also for people not so closely connected to the knowledge economy, such as people who are
best in working with their hands. (We have to suppose that
by that time, the carpenter's work can't be done better by a
robot.)

A piece of the cake

As automation widens its scope of the tasks it can perform,
the greater economic cake to divide increases. The question
is whether we will actually cut up the cake equitably. The
current economic megatrends are not promising: income
inequality is on the rise, and jobs in the middle are under
pressure.

If we all want to keep working and providing for ourselves,
we have to listen to thinkers like Saskia Sassen, who I referred to above, and Thomas Piketty, who in his book *Capital
in the Twenty-First Century* looks critically at the domination
of labour by capital. Globalisation, the neoliberal stress on
individual responsibility, the state of our planet, technological development and the increasing role of money are
making a fundamental discussion of our (economic) future
unavoidable.

How we cut up the cake remains a relevant issue. But who
is holding the knife? While we are having this discussion,
perhaps we can already start to take advantage of the oppor-

tunities offered by the liquid society to create value in a new way. And hopefully we can also make a living.

Opportunities in the middle

At the beginning of this chapter I quoted the Dutch poet Lucebert, whose most famous line of poetry is 'everything of value is defenceless.' This line has been displayed in neon on the façade of an office building in the Dutch city of Rotterdam since the 1980s. In this way, the insurance company that owned the building, had complied with its legal obligation to spend a percentage of the construction cost on art. Such irony: the things that have *real* value, according to Lucebert, can be found 'in the heart of the times', in the here and now, not in an uncertain future against which you want to take out an insurance policy.

Maybe the insurance company is right and we should deny Lucebert and try to make alternative forms of value less defenceless. We could search for new forms of value creation – work, enterprise or others – that counteract the increasing inequality on the employment market, that transform the dangers of technological advances into useful opportunities, and that work not on the basis of impoverishment but enrichment, either in financial terms or otherwise.

After all, what we really want is not to descend to the level of lousy jobs or to live on ever-eroding welfare provided by the state, but to roll up our sleeves and apply ourselves. As an optimist, I believe this is possible.

I will now take a look at four directions for the creation of value in a new way:

• A more flexible way of working offers opportunities for people to regain control of their own work and escape ossified hierarchical forms.

- As proposed by the aforementioned Jaron Lanier, we need
  to try to bring humanism back into the economy by selling
  our own data and ideas at a high price.
- Interesting tasks can be performed by all kinds of new
  middlemen in accordance with innovative business models. You could become a specialised travel agent or sell
  subscriptions as an expert consultant.
- By merging with technology, man can become the fifth robot referred to above: a cyborg that functions better than a
  human being or a machine alone.

Flexible work

You can offer your services online through sites such as
Upwork. Together with other parents, you can work for a day
in a classroom in your children's school. Or log in to your
work's or client's intranet while sitting on the beach. The idea
behind flexible work is that you yourself can organise when
and how you work. Whether this is internationally, national-
ly or locally, as an employee or freelancer.

Frank van Massenhove is the highest-ranking civil servant
at the Belgian Federal Social Security Service. He has said in
an online interview that it would have cost the same to hire a
suite in the Hilton hotel as it did to pay for the office he used
to spend about three percent of his time in. The hot desks
in the Service's great new offices are a visible innovation,
but are by no means the only innovations Van Massenhove
has introduced. Employees assess their bosses, who are also
present in the same physical space. The employees determine their own working hours and where they work; they
can work from home. The result: lower costs for buildings
and travel, increased productivity and more enthusiastic
personnel. Van Massenhove gathered ideas from all over the

world and blended them together to create a unique, revolutionary cocktail.

Belgium is known as a country with much more traditional hierarchies than the Netherlands: there, the boss is usually the boss and that's it. If flexible work has proved possible in such a culture, and at a federal government agency no less, the possibilities elsewhere must be almost limitless.

In the Netherlands, power company Eneco has now introduced flexible work as well. Work at their new headquarters is 'activity-related'. Noone has a permanent desk. Instead, there are areas dedicated to 'standard' work, concentrated work, communication and meetings. Various 'power workshops' were needed to let employees adjust to this new way of working. Some 'golden rules' had to be introduced to regulate this newly found freedom. Likewise, the freedom in Massenhove's government service is also mitigated by some obligations: the employees' duties and responsibilities have been laid down on paper in much greater detail than before.

The examples show that a conscientious implementation of flexible work can not only improve the performance of an organisation, but also make it more attractive to new employees. Highly educated knowledge workers profit from this in particular.

Working locally

Many employees won't mind if their employer asks them to kindly stay away from the office one or two days a week and work from home. This gives freedom and saves on childcare costs. Nevertheless, working from home is not for everyone: there are other distractions such as the washing that needs doing and children who can make it very difficult to really get to grips with that tricky case.

Little wonder then that local, flexible workplaces are springing up everywhere, such as WeWork, which runs 132 locations in 31 cities, including Chicago, Sydney, Berlin, Beijing, London, Amsterdam and Seoul. You'll find an interesting mix of people in any of their spaces. Freelancers go there to get out of the house, to meet inspiring people and have a proper cup of coffee. 'Wage slaves' are also increasingly making use of services like these, allowing them to broaden their perspectives in a different working environment.

These new flexible workplaces are springing up in city centres, along motorways, but also in places that we don't usually associate with work. At Hotel Schani in Vienna, for example, desks and rented workspaces have made their entry into the lobby. This way, the hotel hopes to suit a changing lifestyle, targeting millennials who appreciate a collaborative atmosphere with less of a divide between work and private life. In a similar vein, some schools have introduced 'school sharing', renting out desks for parents to work (and keep an eye on their children in the meantime). It's a win-win situation that benefits both parents and the school.

And the middle?

In the examples given above, flexible work is most suited to people with higher levels of education: almost everyone who works for Van Massenhove's government service has a university degree, and many of the freelancers who do their creative work on their laptops have also completed higher vocational or university level education.

Nevertheless, forms of flexible work could also suit the (lower) middle level, for example the people that have completed intermediate vocational education. Their jobs are on the line. An interesting idea making use of new technology is 'job carving.' Dutch researcher Jouke van Dijk and investigative journalist Wim van de Pol have given examples of this in the Dutch daily *NRC Handelsblad*: 'In the case of the police, the call for "more officers on the streets" can be realised by removing some officers from the desk jobs currently carried out by police officers and combining these in an administrative job for someone with an intermediate vocational education background. Combining the administrative duties carried out by twenty officers into a single new administrative post can in this way free up nineteen officers who can spend a lot more time patrolling the streets and create a few extra jobs for people with intermediate vocational training. A similar scheme could apply to teaching teams in intermediate vocational education, higher vocational education and pre-university education and to groups of professionals in the services or care sector.'[91]

With these forms, you might not immediately think of the autonomous, cappuccino-sipping creative, nor of the high-level civil servant in the lounge at the Ministry, but there is an important parallel: flexible working allows you to reassess and reinvent tasks, aided by technology, and to let go of ossified working patterns.

As the employment market develops, some typical jobs in the middle will be taken over by technology (completely or in part) or be split up into a series of roles and tasks shared by others. These may include the middle manager – autonomous teams will carry out the remaining management tasks once the computer has performed the discipline-related, process-based work. Set against this are the 'savings jobs' described above in which the administrative tasks of 'field workers' with a lower level of education or training are bundled together in a new administrative post in the middle. In this case too, technology will be essential to allow the person with this new job to be effective.

Human economy

The abovementioned Jaron Lanier is a versatile man: he has received training as a computer scientist, he composes music and he is a developer of revolutionary virtual reality applications.

In his book *Who Owns the Future?* he refers to a number of 'humours' – attitudes for looking at the future.[92] Nine of these are sombre: they are based on mass destruction or the replacement of human beings by computers. One is positive: 'information technology of a particular design could help people remain people without resorting to extreme politics.' The latter is Lanier's preferred basic attitude with which to think about the future.

According to Lanier, at present there is something drastically wrong with the way information is valued on the internet. Everything is free: or so it seems. Instead of a customer of – for example – Facebook, you are in fact the product: your data is sold or used for the optimum placement of an advertisement. This system has to change.

Lanier believes such a change in thinking will eventually also be in the interest of the information giants. 'Google might eventually become an Ouroboros, a snake eating its own tail, unless something changes. This would happen when so many goods and services become software-centric, and so much information is "free", that there is nothing left to advertise on Google that attracts actual money. Today a guitar manufacturer might advertise through Google. But when guitars are someday spun out of 3D printers, there will be no one to buy an ad if guitar design files are 'free.' Yet Google's lifeblood is information put online for free. That is what Google's servers organize. Thus Google's current business model is a trap in the long term.'[93]

The alternative is a system in which people pay for information. You will then be not just a social media customer, but also have something to sell. Efficient organisation of micro payments could give individuals something back for their intellectual efforts and their own data.

In other words, Lanier wants to reintroduce humanism into the (online) economy: not focused on the big shareholders in the uncontrollable corporation, but on people. He gives a nice example. Imagine you meet your future husband or wife through an online dating service. Instead of just leaving the site after the wedding, you stay and provide information on your marriage to the service. On the basis of algorithms, this service would then be able to compare the match between you and your partner with those of new customers in an ever more accurate way. These customers will pay for good recommendations and a good match, and you can profit from this in the form of nanopayments – a kind of tiny royalties.

More obvious examples are micro- or nanopayments for reviews on travel websites that prove useful to others, or for videos posted on YouTube – even if the amounts concerned are only a few cents.

In Chapter 5 I discussed aboutthedata.com, the service offered by big data giant Acxiom. This site, still very much in development, gives (at present only American users) the option to view and edit their own data in the database. The potential is there for them by doing so to earn something back from their own data. However limited and commercial, this approach does (to some extent) give data back to the user. It could be the start of citizens taking back control of their own data and being rewarded for it.

The new intermediary

Doing things yourself is one of the mantras of our age. Practicing flexible work you can take control of your working life;

if Jaron Lanier gets his way, we will also get control of our information back as suppliers of this information.

Is there any role left for the classic middleman? Many intermediaries are threatened with redundancy by smart platforms. Record stores are closing in favour of mass online music markets, estate agents are under pressure now that websites can do their job for next to nothing and perhaps just as effectively. Of course, these smart platforms create jobs, but in a very different line of work and in vastly lower numbers.

The process of cutting links from the cain is called 'disintermediation'. This is not a new term, nor is it a new development: the term was used in the financial world as early as 1967, when American consumers were first able to invest directly in securities such as bonds without having to go through a savings account. Now, automation and transparency have led to more middlemen disappearing from the chain in various sectors.

As a frequent traveller, I am particularly interested in the future of the travel industry – a sector that has been transformed by the rise of online intermediaries. My grandparents still went to a travel agent to book a river cruise; I think back with a smile to how, as a student, I spent hours sitting at the office of Kilroy Travels with one of their staff puzzling over the booking process of a multi-city airline ticket.

It actually surprises me that some traditional travel agents still do exist – doesn't everyone book their trips themselves these days? But no, travel agencies do still exist, although the old-style shop on the corner model is in trouble. Technological developments have created a level playing field that is easy to access, making competition intense and margins low.

A new occupation has arisen in this tough market: the specialised, personal travel agent. I spoke to Fred van Eijk, who for eight years has been running a network of freelancers who book special trips for their customers. The network is rapidly expanding and now has more than a hundred affiliated agents. When Fred started out, travel agencies were his biggest competitors, but this is no longer the case: now, it's the internet. People can find and compare trips themselves, so you need to look for added value. Fortunately, transparency and flexibility are leading to such huge ranges of options, many people need help choosing.

Fred stresses that his field of specialisation is small and personal: 'You have to network, hand out business cards and know your customers personally. You have to think smaller.' As a specialist travel agent, you also have to be an entrepreneur: 'Sitting behind a shop window on the High Street waiting for customers doesn't work.'[94]

In the travel world – as in other sectors – the erosion of the middle can clearly be seen. On the one side are the discounters selling all-in packages at rock-bottom prices and the smart platforms linking supply and demand at a low transaction cost. On the other we find the specialist, VIP travel agents. The old-fashioned travel agents or tour operators are subject to former British Prime Minister Margaret Thatcher's adage: 'Standing in the middle of the road is very dangerous. You get knocked down by traffic from both sides.'

A similar development applies to other retail outlets: on shopping streets in cities, you will find discount store next to a Chinese supermarket and a vintage clothing store, whill al the boutique clothing shops cluster together a stone's throw away. In the right neighbourhood, the extremes come together.

Decentralised utilities

I referred above to Eneco, the giant power company that's got its employees used to flexible work. Maybe these employees soon discover it's more lucrative to start up an energy start-up. Four friends in the Netherlands have already done so, and founded Vandebron, an interesting new player on the Dutch energy market. The company allows customers to specify from which sustainable energy supplier they want to purchase their electricity (gas can't yet be supplied in this way). It could be a windmill in the province Zeeland or solor panels in Groningen; it will always be a small, independent and sustainable supplier. Here we see a new intermediary delivering a tailor-made service to its customers: in addition to energy, they get a share in societal change.

In order to contribute to energy transition, you don't need a start-up – you can simply put some solar panels on your roof and supply the energy to the grid.

All said an done, old habits die hard: many national and local government make it hard to engage in these activities autonomously and easily. For example, In the Netherlands generating electricity is taxed. According to members of parliament for the GroenLinks (Green Left) party Liesbeth van Tongeren and Pepijn Vloemans, this is ridiculous: 'The current legislation acts as a brake on innovation and participation by citizens, and keeps energy expensive, vulnerable and polluting. The freedom to generate your own electricity collectively is a major step towards a transition to a sustainable economy. Power to the people.'[95] Other countries create comparable legal and administrative barriers to much needed civil initiative.

The 'power to the people' perspective put forward by the green parliamentarians applies to a more economic activities than the provision of energy. Caring for the sick and elderly, refuse collection and local safety can all be organised at an ever-smaller scale.

In Great Britain, this policy really took off when David Cameron entered number 10, Downing Street. He was depicted on the cover of *The Economist* in 2010 as a radical activist, complete with Mohican haircut. His activism: contracting out government services to small citizens' initiatives.

Here too, decentralisation is the magic word: the old-fashioned middleman is making way for the citizen who can do it for himself.

The business is changing

Disintermediation in the liquid society has unseated many of the old intermediaries. Reinventing your own place in the chain takes courage and creativity and is often only possible if you are prepared to change the rules of the game.

New players are often more specialised and not afraid to tackle a new business model. As a small consultancy firm, instead of offering your customers a broad package at an hourly rate, you could offer them a subscription in a narrow niche area.[96] Small financial services providers are operating better and better on the complex stock market by making resilience and transparency their core business.[97] Some leave the existing monetary system altogether and trade exclusively in bitcoins.

For the new middlemen, technology is often an important side issue: without the right information and communications tools, it would be impossible to play a convincing, effective role as a small, new entrant to the market.

Making things

I once heard sociologist Saskia Sassen say on the radio that the only people that stay in business are those who make something, either with their heads or with their hands. Sassen exactly echoed the categories of Douglas Adams' Golgafrinchans who stayed on their planet. In reality, there is of course no spaceship in which to send all redundant middlemen to another planet. Thank goodness.

But the people in the middle on planet Earth – the members of the middle class, the people with qualifications in intermediate or higher vocational education and the classic middlemen – do face huge challenges. The middle can become more transparent and cheaper – for example thanks to new technological tools. It can also become more expensive, more intensive and more chic, although this may be reserved only for the happy few. The point is not so much that the middle is disappearing, but rather that the middle will be diversified in scale, and has to be precisely tailored to meet individual needs. 'One size doesn't fit all.' And what works today, is outdated tomorrow. The online discount electronics store has its counterpart in the Apple Store; the cheap all-inclusive travel agent is paired with the personal, 24-hour trip advisor.

There is hope for the people, provided that they actively look for new ways of creating value, give up the old certainties and take control.

7

The melting diamond
The end of the middle is the beginning of new power relations

This chapter deals with power. For a long time, power worked according to the pyramid principle, with a clear vertical structure. Leaders at the top, the 'people' at the bottom. But in the liquid society based on the diopticon I introduced in Chapter 4, power is changing along with the rest of society. Autonomy and trust are being redefined. From the once highly self-sufficient Albania we will move through the bitcoin to a Europe of strong regions – the traditional middle always makes way for a smarter, more modern version.

Diamond life

If you want to know how hard something is – for example, a metal – you can carry out the Vickers hardness test. This involves a diamond ground into a pyramid shape being pressed into the substance with great force; the volume of the impression determines its hardness.

The phenomenon of entropy, an important concept in thermodynamics, has hardly any effect on diamonds. This concept from the field of physics represents an increase in chaos.

For a very long time, society has been set up in line with the diamonds and pyramids model, with a high degree of Vickers hardness: people knew their place. The German film *Metropolis* from 1927 effectively depicts this in a surreal, dystopian vision. The workers, condemned to a subterranean existence, march in formation to and from their workplace in the mines. Above the ground, the elite are better off. The film is an artistic representation of one of the excesses of the way society was ordered during the industrial age, many rudiments of which we still see today: groups of schoolchildren thirty to a class, categorised by age, all following the same curriculum; white collar employees working away in their cubicles from nine to five; a hierarchical distribution of tasks between higher and lower-placed government bodies. In at least one respect, the diamond as a substance differs from the social relations it represents: the latter are not always transparent, and get cloudy when time passes.

The melting diamond

The diamond is now beginning to melt: even a hard society, with a persistent, self-reproducing social order, has to move with time. The structuring principle as such is at stake; in the liquid society, relations are very different.

In the previous chapters, I have sketched the developments that play a role herein. Radical transparency provides insights in the processes, organisations, knowledge and the general ups and downs of people's lives. Radical decentralisation allows people to take control of their lives and the world around them at a very basic level. I have put these together in a model I call the diopticon: a situation in which the many can watch the many and quickly enter into relationships with one another (and break these just as quickly). Technology helps with this: in a very literal sense everyone watches everyone else through videos on YouTube, and in a metaphorical sense flexible forms of organisation, global communications flows and innovative forms of entrepreneurship become more real, and become part of our everyday reality.

In the liquid society, time is even more significant: social change is taking place at an ever-increasing pace. As Zygmunt Bauman says: 'Descriptions of fluids are all snapshots, and they need a date at the bottom of the picture.'[98]

Shared money, shared energy

Many of the developments I have sketched until now have a social benefit. For example, the bitcoin and the generation and distribution of electricity. Let me briefly explain the bitcoin: this digital currency, in use since 2009, is a 'cryptocurrency' – a virtual currency made possible by encryption. In the early days of its existence, a hacker ordered a few pizzas for 10,000 bitcoins. Back then, the new virtual currency was not worth the paper it was printed on, being quoted at 0.003 dollars. The bitcoin exchange rate fluctuates (see Figure 7.1), but is worth hundreds of dollars today. The poor hacker probably still has nightmares about those pizzas.

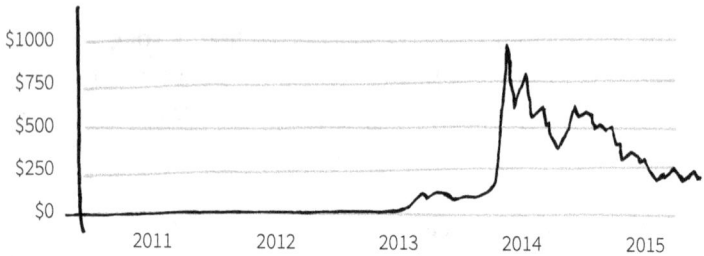

Figure 7.1

Bitcoins are a risky business. They are an investment product for the financially brave. Your hard disk could crash (in that case you cannot retrieve them), the market is volatile and the exchange rate risks are enormous. Brokers go bankrupt and hackers are a constant worry. These hackers could be anywhere – it turned out that the CEO of the bankrupt trading platform MtGox, Mark Karpeles, probably stole hundreds of millions from his own users by using malware to raid the bitcoin wallets of customers.

Nevertheless, it's strange that we make a distinction between virtual money such as the bitcoin and the litecoin and 'real' money such as the dollar and the Swiss franc. Money hasn't been a physical coin for centuries anymore. In fact, the gold standard for the dollar was abandoned in the last century, making money a mere plaything of markets and governments pushing the buttons. Banks had then and still do have a special role: for every Euro put in, they can lend out at least ten. They create money out of thin air. How virtual can you get? Just like before as after the crisis, the banks present successes from the past as guarantees for the future.

Bitcoins are being registered in the 'block chain', a public register simultaneously installed on the computers of all people who have a bitcoin wallet. As a result, all users have a complete copy of the transaction history of every bitcoin, which makes forgery impossible. The maximum number of bitcoins is technically restricted to 21 million. Cryptography on countless computers assures that the currency's mechanism is not accessible to any government or bank that may want to interfere. This has given the bitcoin an incredibly high value against 'real' currencies, but could just as easily collapse like a house of cards if people massively sell their bitcoins. For example, when they exchange them for Chinese renminbis.

The discussion about the bitcoin is interesting. First, what is it that we put our confindence in? Once, we didn't trust anyone at all to create money (transactions were always paid for in hard cash); later, we blindly trusted the government and the banks, although more recently this confidence has taken a painful blow. Perhaps now we will put our faith in anonymous, impersonal, uncrackable cryptography. One striking aspect is that the bitcoin is hardly sensitive to decision-making, power and influence. It is an anarchic currency in the sense that rulers have no instruments of influence, which they do have when it concerns 'real' money (the most they could do is to forbid bitcoins).

Another question concerning this dilemma is: how should public utilities be organised in the twenty-first century? According to American economist Jeremy Rifkin, the production of sustainable energy is booming. He sees two 'uncanny parallels' between the development of the internet and that of energy.[99] First, the development of renewable energy sources is showing an exponential growth in relation to solar and wind energy, while geothermal energy, biomass and water lie ahead. Second, although start-up investments are very high, the marginal costs of producing and distributing energy, like information, are negligible.

According to Rifkin, internet and energy merge into an Energy Internet that will turn the way we generate and distribute energy in society upside down. 'When Internet communications manage green energy, every human being on

Earth becomes his or her own source of power, both literally and figuratively.'[100]

Down with capitalism

Jeremy Rifkin holds that our entire capitalist system will have to be reinvented because of some technologies. He believes in a communications/energy matrix as the infrastructure for a world characterised by extreme productivity. In his book *The Zero Marginal Cost Society* (2014) he criticises the capitalist model, which aims at assigning a monetary value to everything: 'The food we eat, the water we drink, the artefacts we make and use, the social relationships we engage in, the ideas we bring forth, the time we expend, and even the DNA that determines so much of who we are have all been thrown into the capitalist cauldron, where they are reorganized, assigned a price, and delivered to the market.'[101] But it can't go on like this: according to Rifkin, the system has fallen victim to its own success. Due to continuous innovation, the marginal costs – the extra cost per product – approach zero, meaning that market forces, the foundation of the capitalist system, no longer function. He sees this already happening in various sectors: in the entertainment industry, in publishing and communications the reduction of marginal costs has almost put an end to the traditional, profitable model. But it will go much further. 'Within the next two to three decades, prosumers in vast continental and global networks will be producing and sharing green energy as well as physical goods and services, and learning in online virtual classrooms at near zero marginal cost, bringing the economy into an era of nearly free goods and services.'[102]

Rifkin argues that the whole system will change. The principle of *the winner takes all* will have to make way for a more decentralised approach. You still wonder why, even in innovative sectors, so many huge companies currently enjoy success. If Rifkin is right, they should have played their part by now? You would think it's about time to break the chains, make them transparent and smoothen them, so that individuals and small, flexible companies can call the shots, in line with Rifkin's theory.

A powerful challenge

The examples of the bitcoin and the generation and distribution of energy clearly present an opportunity: in the liquid society, radical decentralisation and the required transparency enable us to spend virtual money and heat our homes.

We should also consider power. We have to ask whether we, as consumers and citizens, still have sufficient influence on the essential public utilities. They are an essential lubricant for everything we do, but can become a toy in the hands of parties we don't control.

No household can do without internet, energy and money. Which begs the question if we are really in charge of our own homes, however radically decentralised our lives may be. On all sides, we are surrounded by external power.

Autarchy

Enver Hoxha, an intriguing Cold War figure and leader of Albania from 1944 until his death in 1985, created an ideology out of self-sufficiency. His ideal of the autarchic state plunged his country into deep poverty; he could teach North Korea's Kim Jong-un a thing or two. Personal freedom was worth nothing in that country: citizens were competently spied on and, like Stalin in the Soviet Union, Hoxha closed down most of the churches. Just one old religious village, Berat, was left untouched – probably for opportunistic reasons. In 1968, the villagers expressed their gratitude to their leader by painting the name 'Enver' in 100-metre high white letters on the mountainside. When I visited the village a few years ago, 'Enver' had been changed to 'Never.'

Since Hoxha, autarchy – self-government – has been a dirty word that stands for backward governments that deny their citizens the delights of the global free market and the access to raw materials needed for a good life. Refined oil to put in a car is the simplest example of this. In Albania, the horse and cart were the principal means of transport until the end of the 1980s. In the case of more advanced applications, the required raw materials become more specific; mobile telephones, for example, contain the metals tantalum and tungsten, which are not found lying about just anywhere.

I don't envy living like the Albanians during the Cold War, without car or iPhone. But now the little country is on the up, importing and exporting like there's no tomorrow. Yet at the same time, something else is going on: the concept of autarchy seems to have made a comeback. Self-managing teams replace company managements, groups of citizens organize their own waste collection and provide homes with energy.

An overly simplistic idea of such decentralised, self-managing mechanisms could lose sight of the fact that we all have to take important collective decisions on the infrastructure and the rules of the game. If we don't, someone else will decide for us.

A term related to autarchy could help us out here: autonomy.

Autonomy

I don't own a car, but I do have a driving licence; when I occasionally do get behind the wheel of a rented or shared car, I immediately get a great sense of freedom and maturity – probably because I have not get used to spend long periods sitting in traffic jams every day. In a broader sense, I am very attached to the freedom to go wherever I want. This is about freedom, but also about the more abstract notion of independence: being able to make your own choices in a meaningful way. Apart from being free, I also want to be autonomous.

The great political philosopher John Rawls wrote that man's moral dignity lies in a sense of justice and the ability 'to plan, revise and rationally pursue a conception of the good.'[103] Rawls imagines an 'original position', a thought experiment in which a group of citizens designs the just society from behind a 'veil of ignorance.' The veil means that no one knows his or her social class, race or personal characteristics: citizens deliberate on the basis of their rationality. This means that they will ensure in their design that the worst position in society is still acceptable. For Rawls, this 'original position' represents the autonomy of citizens in a democratic society.

Autonomy is not just the ability to control your own life, which sounds like autarchy, but it is also about taking account of the rights of others and deliberating and taking decisions on significant matters collectively. Autonomy could be seen as the responsible little brother of decentralisation.

International giants

In Chapter 3, I described the activities of the immense technology companies Facebook, Google, Apple and Amazon. Their role in society has become much bigger than that of mere suppliers: they provide a public utility. If we want to take autonomy seriously, we should collectively decide on the conditions that apply to their activities. A similar problem exists in relation to the financial system. There are very few people who feel they can significantly deliberate and take part in deciding about the conditions that apply to the banking world. Our autonomy is in jeopardy – we are no longer the boss in our own homes.

So, there is a problem with the relationship between the people, *demos,* and the home it lives in, *oikos* – the latter being the Greek word from which 'economy' and 'ecology' are derived. In economic terms, this can clearly be seen in the behaviour of companies. They make excellent use of the liquid society: they operate across national borders, settle in several countries at once and choose the most beneficial regime for each of their interests. The declining proportion of tax paid by companies is a good example of this. Apple, for example, hardly paid any tax at all for decades thanks to a construction that became known as the 'double Irish arrangement'; companies are able to shelve their royalties on favourable terms in the Netherlands; and Belgium levies no capital gains tax on the sale of shares. The Dutch may discuss all of these issues until they are blue in the face, but the only decision they can take is to increase their own tax levels, resulting in an exodus of multinationals from the country.

During the 1980s, the Dutch government launched a campaign under the slogan, 'A better environment starts with you.' That was not even true back then – the better environment which did eventually arrive, started with the government tackling acid rain. Decades later, environmental problems are stacking up all around us: the Earth is heating up and a fundamental shift in energy use seems absolutely essential. But not achievable.

The editor-in-chief of *Foreign Policy* hits the nail on the head: 'Traditional systems of social organisation are increasingly ill-suited for our brave new world. Consider the law: Even flexible constitutions like that of the United States weren't built to deal with the issues that would almost certainly be occupying the framers' minds, were they alive today

– like who owns the data we produce, what privacy rights we should have, and whether we are born with an inalienable right to access the Internet. Existing economic models, global alliances, and international institutions are just as poorly equipped for handling the tasks at hand.'[104]

In many different areas, adjustments are needed to prevent our democratic autonomy from becoming an empty phrase. But if we really want to become the boss in our own home again, we have to know where that home is. Is the world our home? Should we organise at a European level? Is the nation state of the Netherlands fit for revival, or should we put our faith in the effectiveness of our urban agglomeration? In the liquid society, we will not be able to escape doing all of this at once, and above all: with one another.

Down with the nation state!

In the classic power pyramid, the nation state is the ultimate middleman. Above it, we find the European Union; below there are the provinces and municipalities. At the national level, countries decide to delegate certain powers up or down. The principle of subsidiarity applies within the European Union: only those matters which cannot be tackled at a national level are arranged at the supranational level. Downwards, national governments can delegate tasks based on the principle of decentralisation: in territorial terms to provinces and municipalities, and in functional terms to the Water Authority, for example.

All fine and well in theory. In practice, national governments have less and less to say. Problems don't stop at national borders: climate change is a global problem – any decisions taken on this in any particular country are at best a drop in the ocean. Big business also takes less and less notice of Munuch, Sofia or Athens. The nation state is increasingly an impotent leftover from the nineteenth-century system of states. The welfare state becomes more expensive all the time, while companies pay less and less tax; borrowing money is a bad idea given the massive levels of national debt, and is also often made impossible by European regulations. The nation state can have little say in the development of the infrastructure of the liquid society: Jeremy Rifkin's Energy Internet, for example, could never be a national project. Europe offers much more possibilities.

Eurotopia

Jean Monnet, one of the founders of the European unification, said that the European project is about cooperation between peoples rather than nation states. One could call him prescient: in the eyes of the spiritual father of the European Community, the days of the nation state may have been counted in the1950s.

Already at the founding of the European Coal and Steel Community, the precursor to the European Union set up in 1951, nation states lost a significant part of their autonomy – namely the ability to individually develop a war industry. Monnet must have known that national politicians would eventually realise that they had lost a lot of power to Europe. And that hurts. But would Monnet have fathomed that in 2014 there would also be a power shift from the nation state to local and regional communities?

Business people have favoured this Europe of the regions for some time now. Freddy Heineken for example: a big European and a big businessman. Originator of the slogan 'Heerlijk, helder, Heineken' ('Lovely, clear Heineken'), he took his business into the Fortune 500. Fifteen years after Freddy's death, Heineken is still one of the top large companies. In his pamphlet *The United States of Europe: Eurotopia?* from 1992 (the year of the Maastricht Treaty), Heineken argued for the division of a stronger Europe into regions on a human scale. In his Eurotopia, Europe is no longer the sum of the member countries, but a conglomerate of regions, each with 5 to 10 million inhabitants. Claiming *small is beautiful*, these regions could bring about economic prosperity and political stability. The biggest threat poses the nation state, striving to represent a nation on anachronistic grounds and thereby blocking efficiency.

The question is whether countries are prepared to give up their last remnants of national pride for something less concrete: an identity as regions in Europe. The supporters of Geert Wilders in the Netherlands, Marine le Pen in France and Nigel Farage in the United Kingdom would not agree.

In the regions, however, people are more enthusiastic. True, in 2014 the majority of Scots voted against independence (by 2,001,926 votes to 1,617,989), but maybe they did so because the Scottish nationalists got what they wanted anyway: an autonomous status within the United Kingdom such as Québec in Canada could only dream of; and fiscal autonomy almost within reach. Many independence movements do see value in Europe. A survey by Durham University and the University of East Anglia carried out in October 2014 showed that, as a majority of constituencies in the United Kingdom would vote for a 'Brexit' in a referendum, such a proposal in Scotland could count on a majority in just four constituencies.[105]

If Scotland, Catalonia, the Basque Country and Friesland were to become independent, they would still be nation states, although on a more 'human scale.' But the most important place in terms of accumulation of new power is the city.

Mayors as world leaders

Boris Johnson is a man of both words and deeds. To begin with the latter: the tousle-haired former Mayor of London managed to get Barclays bank to sponsor London's bike hire plan with tens of millions of pounds. These Barclays Cycle Hire bikes are known as 'Boris Bikes.' They truly go forth and multiply: there are now eight thousand of them.

Nevertheless, 'Bozzer' is more known for his words than his deeds. His panegyric to the city speaks volumes. 'We seek cities because there are a greater range of girls at the bar, of reproductive choice. But above all, talented people seek cities for fame. They can't get famous in the fucking village.' A classic example of one of his politically incorrect quotes or 'Boris bites.' But he has a point. The relevant centre of power is less and less with the national government and more and more with the urban agglomeration.

Globally, and for some years now, more people live in cities than on the countryside. And we don't see this migration to the cities to end yet. The World Health Organisation expects that more than 70 percent of the world's population will be urban dwellers by 2050. That's the equivalent of eight more megacities like New York each year.'[106]

In his book *If Mayors Ruled the World: Dysfunctional Nations, Rising Cities*, American politicologist Benjamin Barber argues for a 'cosmopolis.' According to him, only cities are able to link participation, which takes place locally, to power, which is centralised. Nation states used to do this, but have become too big to support citizenship. Barber talks about 'glocality', a form of cosmopolitism which in effect means you are in two places at the same time: at once very local and very global. In an interview, he said about this: 'A place where you feel you're living locally, in the neighbourhood, but also globally, a place that is deeply connected, both politically and civically, to cities all over the world, to a global economy and a global culture.'[107]

In the Netherlands, the urge for change is increasing: more and more tasks are being devolved to municipalities from central government, but these municipalities are not financially independent. It is about time that regional and urban managers come up with plans to strengthen local government, to improve its control and to involve the population in the increasing role of the smaller administrative unit.

Barber argues for a world parliament of mayors (elected mayors, of course). He is already seeing good examples of cooperation between mayors, for example in the areas of climate change and transport, but, in his view, it is too compartmentalised. Barber is a great advocate of United Cities and Local Governments, an organisation virtually no one has heard of, but which has been running a network of mayors and regional governments from a broad perspective for ten years now. According to Barber, this cooperative organisation has great potential: 'What it lacks is a self-conscious sense of its possibilities for governing, for legislation and for common practices that actually affect behaviour in cities across the world.'[108]

The liquid government

For governments, these developments mean that they will have to adjust their strategies. Internet expert Tim O'Reilly believes that, in the information age, states can no longer present themselves as a counter offering a limited number of options, but as a platform, a 'flourishing bazar' of government services – building blocks others can use.[109] According to Paul Romer of New York University, large companies and government bodies play an equal role as 'platform managers and curators of ecosystems.'[110]

From the middle layer in a power pyramid, the government is becoming an intermediary making the liquid society possible. In the diopticon I described in Chapter 4, the government is just one of the players ensuring that connections can easily be made and just as easily be broken again. In practice, that could mean that rules sometimes have to be applied in a more 'liquid' manner. In Amsterdam-West, an area has now been established in which the zoning plan that prohibits retail and catering establishments from sharing the space has been partly set aside. A good initiative, but perhaps we should go further and not be so afraid of creating an occasional free space such as Christiania in Denmark. The government is criticised from all sides: society is changing so fast, and the decision-making apparatus limps along, out of breath. Individuals and groups have their own concept of the good life and have the energy and ideas to put this into practice but quickly come up against a wall of rules, procedures and structures. The nation state struggles to get to grips with the innovative, decentralised forces in society, and is in danger of becoming irrelevant.

The Empire Strikes Backwards

Change, however necessary, doesn't come about by itself. Political systems are aimed at retaining their structure; within organisations the survival instinct prevents essential changes of course; and people get stuck in their familiar patterns. Old habits die hard.

Changes, however, are unavoidable; there's little point in trying to stop them. The consequences are far-reaching: the middle classes struggle, middlemen in the economy and society get new roles and the nation needs to reconsider its role, too. In the meantime, big global developments and players take up dominant positions on the global stage. The way the cake is cut is still relevant.

This requires tailor-made leadership: a different solution for every problem at the relevant, unique scale. 'One size does not fit all', nevertheless, one scale is always relevant: the human scale. Even in the twenty-first century, man is still the measure of all things.

So, what do we have to do? I mentioned philosopher Peter Sloterdijk above, where I quoted from his book *You Must Change Your Life*. I believe that, whether we want it to or not, we will have to change the way we live.

Moral duties

According to Sloterdijk, you and I will also have to change our lives. But in what direction? What moral duty do thinkers see resting on our shoulders? For a long time, Immanuel Kant's ethical framework was the standard. His first 'categorical imperative' states: you must act in accordance with a 'maxim', a precept that could become a universal law. His second categorical imperative is that man should never be a means, but always the end. According to Kant, both of these imperatives amount to the same thing. But there is one big problem with both of them: they focus so entirely on man that the planet we inhabit is neglected, even though it cannot ' [...] be denied: the sole fact of universal ethical significance in the world today is the diffuse, omnipresent insight that things can no longer go on as they are', as Sloterdijk puts it, describing how the philosopher Hans Jonas stretched the commandment into an ecological imperative: act in such a way that the consequences of your actions are compatible with the continuing existence of real human life on earth. In Sloterdijk's opinion, this still is quite difficult, it entails that one would '... have to become a fakir of coexistence with everyone and everything, and to reduce [her] footprint in the environment to the trail of a feather.'[111] Nevertheless, this is necessary and you and I need to swing into action.

Sloterdijk pleads for an anti-authoritarian culture and in fact, he assumes we live in such a culture.[112] This correctly leads him to make the individual human being the measure of authority. Only if we, as human beings, can look reality in the face and are not tempted to march en masse into the abyss, we do have a chance. That is why the anti-authoritarian human, who incessantly trains himself to create a role for himself, feels more attracted to Obama's slogan 'Yes we can' than to the coercive 'you must' of many activists. We don't like to feel external pressure, but we do like to experience pure spontaneity.

Although Sloterdijk places authority in the final instance with the individual, he is well aware that people are under pressure by all kinds of institutions. Government bodies have always liked to do so, and to this date they are the only ones to have dragged us into senseless wars. Other institutions are now well on the way to take on tasks that were once reserved to governments only, like censorship, imposing rules of decency and monitoring people. Just think of Google and Facebook, for example, and you will see what I mean: with all the virtual police on the digital highway these days, public affairs and the private domain have become inextricably intertwined.

We have an obligation to look critically at institutions. For example, the international financial system, the military-industrial complex and the oil companies. We have to change the world, and we have to change ourselves, within an anti-authoritarian culture that puts man at the centre.

By no means everyone longs for a creativity-based career: we also need people who can build, make and sell things. However, we need to achieve a healthy anti-authoritarian attitude within a liquid society to make use of our talents in a creative way. And that is what I will be discussing in the next chapter.

8

Talent spotting

On management, self-leadership and new forms of capital

In the previous chapters, I have tried to connect the very largest with the very smallest: giant social and technological developments and organisations with the individual doing everything on his own. That middle is being squeezed. In this final chapter, I will track down new forms of leadership, including self-leadership. The watchword in all this is talent: it is only by recognising our qualities and relating to one another that we can be successful.

Most people don't listen with the intent to understand;
they listen with the intent to reply.
Stephen Covey

Anyone can sing

In August 2006, when she was just seventeen, Esmée Denters from Arnhem created a channel on YouTube. She posted videos of herself singing songs. Almost immediately, her fame began to spread like an oil slick; in 2007 various record companies were queueing up to sign her. She recorded a song with Justin Timberlake, toured Scandinavia with him and was a guest on the *Oprah Winfrey Show*. And now? In 2015 she was a contestant on *The Voice UK*, but got eliminated in the third round. Except for this one newsworthy item, little has been heard about Esmée in recent years.

Since *Big Brother*, the TV in your living room (now a flat-screen, of course) has been flooded with talent contests. They have proven a highly lucrative export product for the Dutch entertainment industry, formats with jury members in revolving chairs are sold to all corners of the globe.

Sometimes it seems like everyone wants to be the best – whether it's singing, dancing or baking. But if you listen to the barbed comments from the juries, it doesn't seem that everyone can be the best. Fortunately, most people have more modest talents, and most of these people's ambitions are correspondingly modest.

The challenges and opportunities presented by the liquid society mainly apply to an elite of super-creatives, who control their enormous network from a flexible workstation and perform innovative miracles, and to social and economic leaders who want to equip their organisations for the future. However, the changes that take place in the liquid society are also relevant to a much larger group of citizens and working people who want to earn their keep through a nice job that offers sufficient challenges – but not too many. My neighbour, for example. She works in a department store and has been doing that with pleasure for many years, but fears for her future. The last thing she wants is to be forced to swim around like a free radical in an all-new diopticon.

My hope is that, with this chapter, I will be able to come up with a message equally applicable to the born leader, the creative entrepreneur and my neighbour. The key word here is listening. But I'll start with the management. For decades, it is *the* mechanism for getting higher up the ladder. A situation that is going to change.

The manager in the machine

Office buildings are full of them: organisations that work according to a pyramid structure – the leaders at the top, the managers in the middle and the workers at the bottom. All kinds of management theories are based around the standard structure by famous organisation expert Henry Mintzberg, shown in Figure 8.1. The organisation itself is structured along the lines of a pyramid, with an apex, a middle line and an operating core, and two flanks. The left flank is the techno structure, consisting of the analysts who standardise the organisation (controllers, planners, HR managers) and on the right flank are the support services (from the canteen to, confusingly enough, the ICT department).

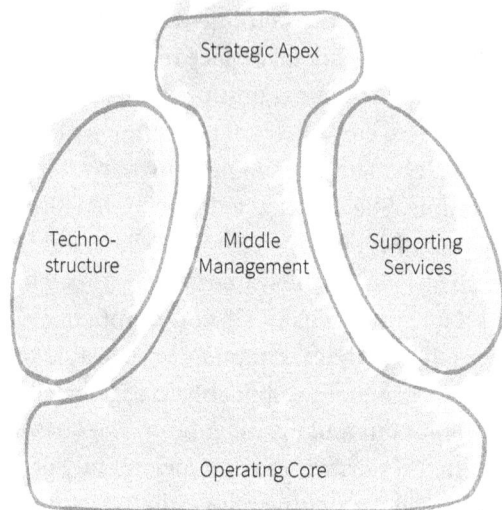

Figure 8.1

Mintzberg distinguishes between four variants of this model, each with more or less emphasis on process, skills and roles.[113] The main structuring principles are always vertical control and the arrangement of an organisation by functions. An interesting fifth variant, of which Mintzberg admits his diagram is less applicable, is the model of 'adhocracy'. 'The adhocracy must hire experts and give power to them. Professionals whose knowledge and skills have been highly developed in training programs. Unlike the professional bureaucracy, the adhocracy cannot rely on the standardized skills of these experts to achieve coordination, because that would cause standardization instead of innovation.'[114]

With this, Mintzberg hits the nail right on the head at quite an early stage (Mintzberg's *The Structuring of Organisations* dates from 1995). Standardisation is particularly risky in the case of increasing change, and this fact is being felt by more and more organisations, even by those who in the past could rely on an established structure.

The problems in the middle

It is particularly the middle managers who are the problem: traditionally they are the link between the creative leadership and the people 'on the shop floor.' They are placed above the shop floor in the hierarchy, whereas the ones on the shop floor are better equipped to point out how the work could be improved. Management should better be seen as a process everyone can contribute to and less as a job or a position. But the involvement of shop-floor level workers can't be brought about when we don't redefine the manager, whose function hasn't changed since the industrial age. This industrial attitude very often is the way things work: the middle manager doesn't get involved in the work of colleagues on the same level, but 'manages' the problems below him or her and tries to keep interference from above to a minimum. This may be a workable concept for a biscuit factory, but it doesn't work for a knowledge-intensive business. According to Mintzberg, the trouble with this kind of 'machine bureaucracy' is that the only way of keeping control is direct supervision. 'This means that extraordinary coordination problems between units "bounce up" the hierarchical stairs to be resolved, until they reach a step from which supervision over all the units concerned is maintained.'[115] Thus the management is kept nice and busy.

Many tasks carried out by the traditional middle manager are more service-oriented than control-oriented: shape processes and keep them going. Especially this area can be helped by technological solutions, and make this expensive intermediary layer (partly) redundant.

Technology offers a solution

Do you know Dilbert, that little IT man who works in a terrible office and constantly collides with the management? His tie is always stuck up and his glasses cover his eyes completely.

The author of that cartoon, Scott Adams, keeps a blog in which he discusses in greater detail the issues he satirises in his cartoons. He believes rightly that the important employees who are made redundant by automation are in fact the managers. After all, project management involves fairly simple things: how to spend your budget, how to make sure this actually happens and that the people who need some encouragement get it at the right time. But does a computer programme have sufficient leadership qualities to carry out these tasks? Adams' answer to this question is as follows: 'I would point out that most humans in management have zero leadership skills, so the bar isn't set high.' We are not talking about Steve Jobs here, but rather that irritating middle manager who runs about like a headless chicken acting important. Unlike him, the robot is completely objective and can 'be a hard-ass jerk as often as that is called for.'[116]

Technology can do much of the things the manager used to do. Technology can map out the performance of an organisation and even draw up simple reports. For teams, technology offers opportunities for self-management while retaining transparency. It's hard for the expensive middle manager to compete against a computer: the computer won't leave to join a competitor, won't ask for extra days off and of course it's less expensive. Particularly now that people are much more mobile on the employment market and no longer work for one company for many years, the manager is more and more an all-round professional – and therefore easier to replace.[117]

Circles and horizontal organisations
In a recent blog, Mintzberg drew a diagram (see Figure 8.2)[118] different from his famous pyramid. In this one, the man-

agement is divided into circles. He believes that there is still
a place for a middle – no longer in terms of a hierarchical
middle, but based on a horizontal connection between the
operation and the core: 'Between the central managers and
the operating managers are the *connecting managers*. They
still translate between the centre and the operations, but
also carry the best ideas generated in the operations to the
centre. No longer, like Sisyphus, do they have to do this up-
hill.' The pyramid has tipped over; the organisation becomes
horizontal.

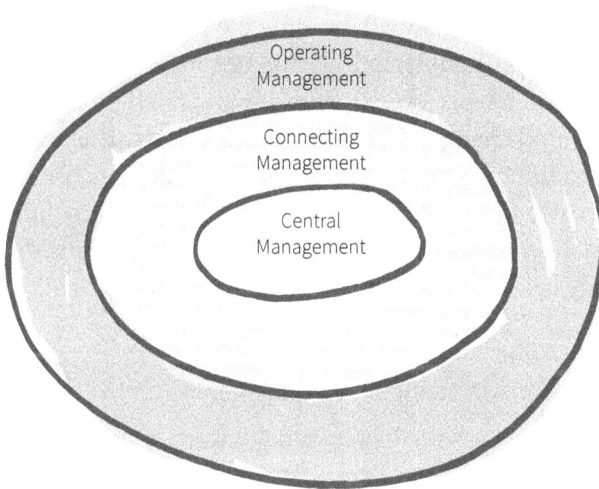

Figure 8.2

In a horizontal organisation, there is no longer any stimulus
to climb the ladder – after all, there is no ladder anymore.
From an inward-looking hierarchical bureaucracy, an agile,
outward-looking organisation develops which sees the world
around the organisation. This world is principally populated
by customers, but if you open a window all sorts of things
can fly in – the wishes, needs and ideas of others will penetrate the walls of your organisation.

Holacracy

In Chapter 4, we've discussed a new way of structuring organisations: holacracy (meaning *kratos*, 'power', to the *holon*, the circle within which people are active.) I will briefly sum up the thought process behind this form of structuring: an organisation no longer is a hierarchy, but consists of circles. Everyone is a member of several of these circles, which are linked. Managing processes are not nailed down in a fixed job description, but are allocated to people when problems have to be solved or tasks performed. These circles can easily be created and broken again.

Whether holacracy will become the new mantra or whether another philosophy will work better, in any case, organisations will have to organise flexibly and open their windows to the rapid changes that take place in society. The people who traditionally pull the strings will lose influence and power, which will shift to others. Companies are no different in this respect from non-profit organisations, and this is equally true of the private sector and the government.

Flow

Middle managers are having a tough time: if their tasks have not already been automated, their jobs could disappear and their tasks redistributed to people on the shop floor. Or you could turn it around: linking up the knowledge 'on the shop floor' with leadership demands qualities and efforts that are essential in order to continue to innovate and make use of talent in the best possible way within organisations.

The latter has been stated by Ikujiro Nonaka, for example: a management guru who in 2008 was named by *The Wall Street Journal* as one of the most influential business thinkers. Together with Ryoko Toyama and Toru Hirata, he wrote a book called *Managing Flow*. It was published in 2008, but has lost none of its relevance in the meantime. The book is geared to knowledge-intensive businesses, but the insights it provides go further and fit perfectly with the liquid society and the diopticon as I described in this book. Nonaka states that, in an organisation that creates knowledge, leadership is not about rigid administrative control but a flexible distribution of managerial tasks in which the leader is determined by the context.[119] At first sight, this fits quite well with holacracy, but the emphasis is different and Nonaka's thinking envisages a role for middle management (which is probably not so surprising given the hierarchically ordered structure of society in Japan).

Nonaka's in-depth analysis of knowledge is particularly interesting. Like the ancient Greek thinker Aristotle, he distinguishes three different forms of knowledge. *Episteme* is universally valid, scientific knowledge; *techne* is technical knowhow based on skills, and finally there is *phronesis*: practical wisdom nourished by experience. The crux is to link dry, impersonal facts (such as financial data) to the reality of the people who work in your organisation. According to Nonaka and his co-authors, an essential capability of a leader is the ability to cultivate phronesis in others.

In my opinion, the term phronesis is extremely apt to account for the role people play in change and leadership. Above, I described technology's tendency to take over more and more tasks from people – and this includes middle management, as I have shown. You don't need an expensive manager to map out and guide processes: this can largely already be done by ever-smarter technology. Nevertheless, human leadership is still required to create the fertile conditions in which these can flourish. In a world that is changing radically, and often in unpredictable ways, leadership, vision and dialogue are essential. Nonaka applies this to knowledge-intensive businesses, but I firmly believe that his message is more broadly applicable. So, I look to the economy in a broader sense, and this leads me to the concept of talentism.

Production factor talent

In Chapter 3, I quoted Brian Gentile, who wrote in *Forbes* that the new production factors (alongside capital) are information and time. In other words: to create value – which is what a production factor does – information (or knowledge) and the speed with which you are able to apply these are of the greatest importance. They are in fact even more important than the two traditional production factors (alongside capital): labour and land.

Poor people! Has homo sapiens, always ready to roll up his sleeves, now been pushed out of the equation altogether by capital, time and information? I don't think so: people are still of the greatest importance. It's just that the term 'labour' no longer fits. 'Talent' gets us much further: it focusses on people rather than the output of their actions. If you are talking about automation, the right question is not 'how can we prevent robots from stealing our jobs?' but rather 'how can we make the best possible use of human talent, in such a way that both man and the collectives in which he operates benefit?' The individual talents of people will play an ever-greater role not only in the most knowledge-intensive organisations, but in society as a whole. In economic terms: a shift is taking place from labour as a production factor to talent as a production factor.

Talentism

The World Economic Forum is an influential, independent body that promotes public-private cooperation and is most well-known for its annual meeting of CEOs from the biggest companies in the world, politicians, intellectuals and journalists. Its founder, chair and driving force since 1971, Klaus Schwab, opened the annual conference in Davos in 2012 with a striking speech in which he went even further than what I have described above. According to him, talent, a word he uses synonymously with creativity, will take over from capital as the most crucial production factor. 'Talentism is the new capitalism' were his words. 'Capital will be superseded by creativity and the capacity to innovate – and therefore by human talent – as the critical factor in production.' According to Schwab, capitalism is not dead (otherwise he would of course have been laughed out of the building by his audience), but it faces some serious shortcomings. Sticking to the present course could lead to a dystopia – an inverted utopia, plunging us into a downwards economic spiral, social strife, protectionism, nationalism and populism. In Schwab's view, the excesses of capitalism should therefore be ameliorated through good social policy and regulation, and the focus on 'cash' should shift to 'creativity.' The sturdiness of the economy and businesses depends not so much on access to capital, but on their success in making use of the innovative, creative power of people: i.e., talent.

The problem is that economic prosperity is still linked to economic growth, which in the developed economies has been declining fairly rapidly. Even in China, growth figures for some years have not been as spectacular as they were.

I believe that growth of talent offers far better prospects, even though talent is quite neglected in most economic theorising, at both macro and micro levels. The balance sheets of companies, the most important indicators of what they are worth, usually make no mention whatsoever of their greatest asset: human capital. Bricks and mortar, inventory, credit and machines are all listed, and these are of course necessary for businesses to operate, but they offer no guarantee for success. Human capital *cannot* be traded (well, it is extremely difficult), it changes constantly, but it forms the heart of the effectivity of an organisation nonetheless.

HR consultancy giant Mercer, which cooperates with the World Economic Forum, has cited the 2013 report *Talent Ris-*

ing. According to the consultants, the gap between the needs of companies and the supply of talent is getting wider all the time: worldwide, 200 million people are jobless, whereas a third of the employers can't find good workers. The report draws a number of interesting conclusions. For example, the BRICS countries (the emerging economies of Brazil, Russia, India, China and South Africa) are not doing so well in this respect: serious obstacles have to be overcome in order to tap creativity. This is striking, because in recent decades it is precisely in these countries that capitalism has performed above average!

Who profits from talent?

During the last century, most European countries have built up quite an extensive welfare state that acts as a social safety net. The underlying idea was very decent, but seen from the perspective of talent as a production factor, it's going quite the wrong way. Tax revenues from work and income have risen significantly in recent decades, but businesses pay an ever-smaller contribution. In October 2014, it was announced that Facebook had paid just 4,327 Pounds Sterling in corporation tax in the United Kingdom.[120] No, there are no zeros missing from the end of that sum: the company literally paid just a few thousand Pounds in tax, less than the average individual employee of that company paid in income tax. This same company wants to open a new headquarters in London in 2017 at the chic address Rathbone Square, and in 2014 it made a global profit of 2.9 billion dollars – twice the figure of the previous year.

The Facebook example is extreme, but it represents the ever-lower tax burden on companies in Europe. The contribution of companies to the collective pot has dropped in just a few decades from 30 to 10 percent[121], while the share paid by labour has increased. The European Commission currently investigates the agreements of companies with various countries to spread their financial transactions in an international patchwork that is favourable to them, thereby reducing their tax liability almost to zero.

We started this chapter with expressions of creativity, but have ended up back at global financial relations of the kind Thomas Piketty has brought into question. Neither you nor my neighbour have read his book, but is the content of his criticism relevant to your lives and my argument? I suspect that it is, both at the highest level of the system as in the smallest details. Global structures should be made fairer and you and your neighbour will both have to come up with better ways of making use of your individual talents. In other words: there is no ready-made bed for either the global economy or the individual citizen of the world.

Basic income as a way of guaranteeing talent development

A welfare state, to a considerable extent funded by businesses (i.e.: taxes on capital and business) can certainly contribute to people to get the best from themselves.

A far-reaching solution that has been frequently put forward is the basic income. The idea behind this is simple: give everyone a reasonable subsistence minimum, but ensure that there is always a stimulus to work or innovate and earn more. At first sight, this may seem like the opposite of the belief that 'everyone should take care of himself' and more like an extreme, simplified form of social safety net for the weakest. A characteristic of the changing economic reality is that the argument for a basic income increasingly focuses on the vulnerable group in the middle: people in the middle-income bracket, who traditionally carried a heavy burden and whose jobs are increasingly insecure.

Three things strike me in particular about the renewed discussions concerning the basic income. First they prove that some solutions end up tackling problems other than those they were initially aimed at (the basic income, originally seen as a simplified social security net for the very weakest, could end up proving effective at relieving pressure on those in the middle). Second, this discussion shows that, from wherever you look at it, the welfare state becomes unaffordable given the low rates of taxation on businesses and capital: both in the case of the basic income and the current system, businesses will have to pay more. Third, this recurring discussion shows that we shouldn't be afraid of big ideas and new ways of organising our political systems.

Big changes in the global financial system and the introduction of a basic income are, much to my regret, not just around the corner: the existing institutions involved in value creation in the form of money are extremely conservative.

However, if the proponents of talentism are right, new forms of value creation should already be approaching, outside of the financial system. And indeed, this is the case. In addition to talent and social interaction, these include things we have been familiar with for a long time: reputation and social capital.

Reputation as capital

In his book *The Tipping Point*, Malcolm Gladwell defined modern change agents as *connectors, mavens* and *salesmen*. Connectors know lots and lots of people, mavens possess a huge amount of knowledge and salesmen are really good at selling. What makes the rise of LinkedIn, Facebook and Twitter so interesting is that everyone has the opportunity to play these roles online, and thereby build up an online reputation. Whereas just a few years ago this reputation would have still had mainly virtual significance, nowadays it becomes increasingly entwined with reputations in the real world.

The American company Klout has now launched the Klout Score, a number between 0 and 100 that shows how well you perform on social media. It is based on your knowledge and skills, the way you share these and how many people respond to this. 'Klout helps people who want to be great at social media,' is how the website puts it. Barack Obama has a Klout Score of 99. This high score is one of the factors that explained his electoral success: he was able to mobilise millions of people through social media. Investor Warren Buffett ('Warren is in the house!') gets 87 points. The Pope, whose Twitter activity I talked about in the first chapter, also has a decent score. According to a blog, he occupies the eighteenth place with a score of 85.

The Klout Score is a product from a commercial company and subject to a lot of ifs and buts. Many more of such aggregated reputation evaluators exist, as well as many sites (like Airbnb) which rank the reputations of their users.

Your reputation is becoming economically more and more important. If you make a complaint to your mobile supplier, consider yourself warned: there are whispers that customer services departments help people with a higher score first. Things get more serious if you want a loan. The site lenddo.com is an alternative to Klout, but works largely on the same principles. This platform determines – on the basis of your online reputation – whether you can borrow money. If you don't pay it back, your extensive network could come to know it. In the end, your ability to support yourself could depend on your score.

Personal reputation and identity are becoming ever more valuable – a logical development in the internet economy, in which the roles of consumer and producer are becoming combined in the 'prosumer.' But although advertisers and sellers are making smart use of the reputation economy, reputation capital is still often a largely untapped resource within organisations and in education.

Social capital

Alongside talent and reputation, I should mention a third form of capital that rightly creates agitation among sociologists and political thinkers: social capital. The American professor Robert Putnam describes it in his book *Bowling Alone*: 'Whereas physical capital refers to physical objects and human capital refers to the properties of individuals, social capital refers to connections among individuals – social networks and the norms of reciprocity and trustworthiness that arise from them. In this sense, social capital is closely related to what some have called "civic virtue." The difference is that "social capital" calls attention to the fact that civic virtue is most powerful when embedded in a network of reciprocal social relations. A society of many virtuous but isolated individuals is not necessarily rich in social capital.'[122]

The title of Putnam's book clearly indicates that he is not greatly satisfied with the state of social capital. Back in the day, Americans went bowling en masse and played in organised matches – these days, you sometimes see people bowling all on their own. Old forms of civic engagement are losing importance. Social capital is on the slide.

I don't share Putnam's pessimism. America's bowling tradition might be fading, but all kinds of new social interaction ensure the cohesion and confidence in society, the importance of which Putnam rightly underlines. His view is shared by Michael Schudson, also an American and, as I would imagine, a big fan of The Simpsons. In the article 'The Varieties of Civic Experience'[123] he describes how civic engagement can take on many different forms, and uses the members of that fictional family as examples: each member of the family in the animated series shows commitment in his or her own way. Homer Simpson is an old-fashioned member of a political party and sticks to this. Marge is the morally aware citizen who will not, however, man the barricades. Lisa is the well-informed, citizen activist. Bart stands for the anti-authoritarian, individualistic citizen who cries about when his interests are threatened. What kind of civic engagement baby Maggie Simpson will show, remains to be seen.

Almost ten years have now passed since Schudson published his article. Baby Maggie would be a teenager by now – if she wasn't stuck being a baby on TV. She is of course a digital native and without knowing, she contributes to the creation of social capital every day. She may be a fervent blogger, a civil journalist posting critical videos, a 'selectivist' who sometimes clicks on things she considers important or signs a petition. There is not much room at school for these new forms of social capital, and when Maggie enters the world of work the only way she may be able to use this is by creating a Facebook page for the staff outing.

Social capital is an engine for change. It is very important to ask yourself every now and then to what and to whom the group, in which social capital is accumulated, relates.

In this context, Putnam wrote an authoritative article in 2007 on the basis of 30,000 questionnaires, concluding that confidence decreases as ethnic diversity increases. This implicates that, in diverse neighbourhoods, there is mistrust between (and also within) ethnic groups, which makes people withdraw 'like a tortoise into their shells.' These insights have found their way into countless reports and essays, but are now outdated. An overview survey from 2009 showed that this is not the case in the Netherlands: no negative correlation was found between diversity and social cohesion; poverty, however, did clearly show a negative relationship with social cohesion. In November 2015, an article in the *American Journal of Sociology* also demonstrated that

Putnam had made errors and should not have drawn these conclusions just so quickly.

Although diversity doesn't seem such a bad idea after all, and even represents a social reality, this social reality is far removed from the utopian view of the world I had when I was at primary school, the 'house of ideals' I discussed in Chapter 5. This presented the world as green, cohesive and even realizable: you can solve problems, only if you want to. Although I am an optimist by nature, I do believe that a new form of cooperation is needed.

Four leadership trends

Talent, reputation and social capital depend on a good environment in order to flourish. They are nurtured by (self-) leadership. Let me point out four trends that will influence leadership:

1. The future leader is not a manager. I see management and leadership more as roles performed by individuals, in different contexts, than as positions in a hierarchy.
2. The future leader is supported by automation. Like the computer programme Vital with its seat on the Board of Deep Knowledge Ventures (see Chapter 6), the combination of man and machine will play an increasingly powerful role in leadership. Vital underlines that, in the era of big data, big uncertainty and big change, decision-making is no longer possible without the intelligence of machines.
3. The future leader is female. In the same way man and machine will have to work together to achieve optimum results, men and women will, too. This is not so much about the gender of the person concerned, but more about making use of diversity. *Harvard Business Review* surveyed 64,000 people about what they saw as the most important competences of modern leaders, and whether these could

be typified as male or female. Eight out of ten (expressiveness, future-orientation, fairness, loyalty, flexibility, patience, intuition and cooperation) were seen as female and just two (decisiveness at number 3 and resilience at number 8) were seen as male. *The Financial Times* reported that female managers of investment funds performed better than men – in that newspaper's opinion because women are more risk-adverse and more likely to stick by their decisions in turbulent times. Whether this is true or not, in any event the classic boss (male or female), whose job description and attitudes date from a time when men made the decisions, will soon be put out on grass.

4. You are the future leader. Whether you are a creative at an advertising agency, a primary school teacher or a cleaner, the job for life and all the benefits it entails will definitely be the exception rather than the rule. For more people, it will be necessary to show leadership in the way they manage their lives and careers. To keep sailing through stormy weather, you need to maintain a good course – and to do this, you have to take control.

This fourth trend is the most important, and the most difficult. In Chapter 5, I introduced a new 'swimming certificate' to try to prevent people drowning in the liquid society – I would now like to add a simple, practical point to this. A point I believe is highly relevant to you, your neighbour, the multicultural society and every organisation.

Learn to listen

In 2012, I took part in a panel discussion as part of the Picnic event. These discussions often go like this: the moderator goes around the group to size up the different opinions, and as a panellist you think up something smart to say when the previous person still speaks, or even better: a joke that will score with the other panellists and get the audience on your side. In such cases, really listening and responding to another panel member doesn't happen; people just talk at one another.

But this discussion, chaired by philosopher Humberto Schwab, was different. His Socratic discussion had a number of interesting rules that were new to me. During the discussion, you could say what you wanted, but only when it was your turn, and you had to be able to repeat the last sentence spoken by the previous speaker. If you were unable to do so, you weren't allowed to speak. The moderator could also ask you to summarize the last fifteen minutes of the discussion; again, if you were unable to do so, you had to keep silent.

The effect of these rules was tremendous: because I was forced to listen, it wasn't possible to gather my thoughts and shut out what the others were saying, even for a moment. I was able to make a joke, but only spontaneously and in line with that which the previous speaker had said.

The question was: why do people do things for others without asking for something in return? This question was eventually refined into: what is a good life? According to Humberto Schwab, the most relevant question there is.

Afterwards, it struck me how massively different this was from discussions without these rules. In spite of all the means of communication at our disposal, it seems that something as basic as listening can't be taken for granted. In short: just listen properly to your neighbour – it will make you and your neighbour much more relevant.

Afterword

Sing to me of the man, Muse, the man of twists and turns
driven time and again off course, once he had plundered
the hallowed heights of Troy.
Many cities of men he saw and learned their minds.
Homer: The Odyssey, translated by Robert Fagles

The myth of Prometheus and Epimetheus

In one of Plato's famous dialogues, which he places in the mouths of Socrates and his contemporaries, Socrates issues an invitation to the philosopher Protagoras. He talks about virtues – how to learn to be a good person for others – and starts with a myth about the qualities of people and animals. He tells us how, in the beginning, there were only gods: mortal beings had not yet been created. Prometheus and Epimetheus were given the task of assigning qualities to both animals and people. Epimetheus volunteered to start, and Prometheus to correct him. In Benjamin Jowett's translation: 'Thus did Epimetheus, who, not being very wise, forgot that he had distributed among the brute animals all the qualities which he had to give, and when he came to man, who was still unprovided, he was terribly perplexed. Now while he was in this perplexity, Prometheus came to inspect the distribution, and he found that the other animals were suitably furnished, but that man alone was naked and shoeless, and had neither bed nor arms of defence. The appointed hour was approaching when man in his turn was to go forth into the light of day; and Prometheus, not knowing how he could devise his salvation, stole the mechanical arts of Hephaestus and Athene, and fire with them (they could neither have been acquired nor used without fire), and gave them to man. [...] And in this way man was supplied with the means of life. amazo'

Man is by nature a technical being, although he is not very good at dealing with power. Thus far, the myth gives a pretty good insight into the contemporary human condition. We control the resources of our planet using our technologies, but we are unable to distribute these fairly. This condition threatens our very survival. If only Michel de Montaigne, possibly the first modern philosopher, had been proved right: 'Are they not dreams of human vanity, to make the moon a celestial earth, there to fancy mountains and vales, as Anaxagoras did? There to fix habitations and human abodes and plant colonies for our convenience, as Plato and Plutarch have done? And of our earth to make a luminous and resplendent star?'[125] It may surprise you that Montaigne wrote this prescient text back in the sixteenth century; it would be another four hundred years before our earth would indeed light up like a strange star in the firmament. She truly does, thanks to all the radio waves in the ether from the TV programmes you watch, the telephone conversations you have and the blogs you read.

Doomsday scenarios

In 2011, I presented a series of broadcasts for the Dutch television channel Human about major philosophers under the

title *Dare to Think* (in Dutch: *Durf te denken*). Each episode
focused on a particular philosopher. Michel de Montaigne
proved to be a very interesting one, an innovative writer
whose works are still an excellent read today. His acute
self-reflection and introspection broke with the traditional
idea that philosophy is the realm of the search for eternal,
immutable truths and realities. Montaigne just tells you
that today he ate a plate of dates, not because of the dates of
course, but because of every human being's search to test
himself or herself and become a better person. My guests in
the programme were convinced that today Montaigne would
be a blogger. He wrote about himself, a popular subject
among contemporary bloggers, as well as what was going on
around him. In his era, the Renaissance, there was quite a bit
going on. The New World had just been discovered and was
bringing new riches and new insights to the happy few. 'The
inhabitants of Mexico were more developed and technically
proficient than the other peoples there. They therefore also
believed, as we did, that the world was coming to an end,
and saw the devastations we wrought upon them as a sign of
this.'[126]

Montaigne seems to see a correlation between the relative technical development of a people and ideas about
the End of Days: doomsday scenarios as a naïve side-effect
of progress. It is an interesting thought which at first sight
seems plausible, certainly if you watch programmes such as
Discovery Channel's *Doomsday Preppers*. This shows how
people are preparing for all kinds of catastrophic disasters
that will mean the end of society as we know it: zombies,
natural disasters or acts of God (or the government). The
year 2012 was a particularly good one for the series: the
Mayan calendar was supposed to end on 21 December of
that year, and sect leaders and gurus decided that this meant
the end-game for the entire human race. A hype in the press
ensued and horror and science fiction authors had a field

day. Fortunately, it all turned out to be fiction. Now, some prophets of doom have said that, although they may have got it wrong last time, the end of the world *really* is nigh.

Doomsday Preppers is in good company: even the great physicist Isaac Newton is said to have prophesized the end of the world (in 2060). In any case the grandfather of classic mechanics paid much attention to the matter. The Newton Project at the University of Sussex, which aims to collect all of Newton's writings and put them online, has already surpassed six million words. A surprisingly large amount of this deals with alchemy and religiously inspired texts which these days would immediately be labelled 'occult.' In scientific terms, Newton was far ahead of his time, and it is actually for this reason he is referred to as the 'last magician.'

I think such doom scenarios have always been with us. Bosch painted the Last Judgement with great imagination in the fifteenth century, Newton believed all kinds of things about the same Last Judgement in the eighteenth century, and in our own century there are people who think the Earth is about to crash into the unseen planet Niburu.

Technical progress is in any event not a quick remedy for superstition and pseudo-science. In fact, the ready availability of information (correct or incorrect) and the spread of ideas through social media have given many superstitions and conspiracy theories powerful ways of reaching new audiences. In this respect, Montaigne's comment has come true, even if the sixteenth-century thinker could never have foreseen it.

Optimistic

I am an optimist, the fact that I have described so many dangers and pitfalls in this book notwithstanding: the big technology companies threatening to crush the individual consumer, an unfair global financial system, the pressure on the middle incomes and the armies of ever more versatile robots looming on the horizon (and other forms of automation) that threatening to take over human manual work and thought. Add to these global poverty, conflicts and climate change and it seems to be getting ever more difficult to look towards the future with confidence.

Nevertheless, I manage it. I make a distinction between superstitious doom scenarios and warnings that we as a species are pushing at our limits and taking enormous risks. The climate is warming up, fuel and raw materials are finite and sooner or later exponential growth has to come to an end. What we need are intelligent solutions; possibly even a radical change of course. I hope that I have been able to contribute to this in some way with this book.

Farid Tabarki,
spring 2016

Acknowledgements

The list of people I would like to thank for their contribution to this book is endless. Every conversation I have had with absolutely everyone, wherever in the world, over the past few years has contributed to my understanding of the transformation taking place in our society and what this means for the position of the 'middle.' I would therefore like to thank you all from the bottom of my heart for all these conversations.

In addition, various interns, friends and acquaintances have thought about and worked on this book. Their contributions also deserve a huge thank you. Two people in particular played a very special role in the creation of this book. During the dinner at the end of 2012 to mark the presentation of the book *Agents of Change: Strategies and Tactics for Social Innovation* I had the pleasure and privilege of sitting opposite Thieu Besselink. The idea for this book was born during my conversation with him. Thank you, Thieu.

Finally, thanks to the research carried out and texts provided by Rindert de Groot this book didn't stay just a good idea, but actually got written. My thanks to you is huge!

About the author

Farid Tabarki is the founding director of Studio Zeitgeist, and has been investigating the (European) zeitgeist since 2000. Topics into which he and his studio undertake research and which set the themes of his many lectures include radical decentralisation, radical transparency and the rise of the liquid society. The studio uses these insights to inspire and help change many (internationally operating) organisations through lectures, seminars publications and debates.

Farid publishes a weekly column in *Het Financieele Dagblad*, a Dutch daily newspaper focusing on finance and the economy. In 2012 he received the Trendwatcher of the Year Award for 2012-2013. He has also presented the TV programmes MTV's *Coolpolitics* and *Durf te denken: Van Socrates tot Sartre*. He is a popular keynote speaker, chairperson and moderator. According to Dutch morning newspaper *de Volkskrant*, Farid is one of the two hundred most influential people in the Netherlands (and the youngest person on the list).

He is also vice-chair of the supervisory board of Het Nieuwe Instituut – architecture, design, e-culture – and a trustee of leadership centre De Baak. He was a member Onderwijs2032, commissioned by the Dutch government, this platform presented a vision of Dutch education policy moving towards the year 2032. Last but not least, Farid is a true world traveller: he plans to visit all the countries of the world. The counter currently stands at 135, so with 63 to go he has more than two-thirds under his belt.

Notes

Chapter 1

1. M. Jongsma, 'Analisten voorspellen nog slechter dan het toeval', *Het Financieele Dagblad*, 29 October 2013. https://fd.nl/frontpage/mensen/626140/analisten-voorspellen-nog-slechter-dan-het-toeval

2. M. Jongsma, 'Analisten voorspellen nog slechter dan het toeval', *Het Financieele Dagblad*, 29 October 2013. https://fd.nl/frontpage/mensen/626140/analisten-voorspellen-nog-slechter-dan-het-toeval

3. Josephine McKenna, 'Vatican Bank Profits Tumble as Pope Francis Orders an Overhaul', Religion News Service, 8 July 2014. https://www.washingtonpost.com/national/religion/vatican-bank-profits-tumble-as-pope-francis-orders-an-overhaul/2014/07/08/e94c85e4-06cd-11e4-9a71-264773a2ffc8_story.html?utm_term=.ebb276f8aed9

4. Kashmira Gander, 'Pope Francis "Furious" at Senior Cardinal Tarcisio Bertone's Plan to "Retire in Four-Storey Penthouse"', *The Independent*, 2 June 2014. http://www.independent.co.uk/news/world/europe/pope-francis-furious-at-senior-cardinal-tarcisio-bertones-plan-to-retire-in-four-storey-penthouse-9470840.html

5. David Gibson, 'Analysis: Pope Francis' Plan for Reform: Convert the Church', Religion News Service, 5 March 2014. https://www.washingtonpost.com/national/religion/analysis-pope-francis-plan-for-reform-convert-the-church/2014/03/05/9d70f9ae-a4a6-11e3-b865-38b254d92063_story.html

6. Maddie Borg, 'Lady Gaga's earnings: $59 Million in 2015', Forbes.com, 29 June 2015. http://www.forbes.com/sites/maddieberg/2015/06/29/lady-gagas-earnings-59-million-in-2015/#14e9dff892d5

7. Neal Pollack, 'How Lady Gaga's Manager Reinvented the Celebrity Game with Social Media', *Wired*, May 2012. http://www.wired.co.uk/article/troy-carter

8. Josh Constine, 'Lady Gaga's Backplane Crashes, Burns Money, Tries To Rise Again', techcrunch.com, 6 March 2015. https://techcrunch.com/2015/03/06/the-backplane-black-box/

9. Steven Bertoni, 'Spotify Sees Jump In Paying Customers With 10 Million Premium Subscribers', *Forbes*, May 2014. http://www.forbes.com/sites/stevenbertoni/2014/05/21/spotify-sees-jump-in-paying-customers-with-10-million-premium-subscribers/#4d0b86051a4c

10. Ian Leslie, 'Kodak vs Instagram: This Is Why It's Only Going to Get Harder to Make a Good Living', *New Statesman*, 28 January 2014. http://www.newstatesman.com/politics/2014/01/kodak-vs-instagram-why-its-only-going-get-harder-make-good-living

11. 'Tot 2017 zal de ontwikkeling van Akademgorodok ruim 30 miljard roebel aan investeringen opleveren', baikal24, 24 December 2011. http://baikal24.ru/text/24-12-2011/2017/

12. Brett Forrest, 'The next Silicon Valley: Siberia', *Fortune Magazine*, March 2007. http://archive.fortune.com/magazines/fortune/fortune_archive/2007/04/02/8403482/index.htm

13. Rick Aristotle Munarriz, 'Mickey Mouse Is Watching You: Does Disney's MyMagic+ Know Too Much?' *Daily Finance*, 10 January 2013. https://www.aol.com/article/2013/01/10/disney-world-mymagic-wristband-rfid-privacy/20423975/

14. Zygmunt Bauman, *Liquid Modernity* (Cambridge: Polity Press, 2000).

Chapter 2

15. Benedictus de Spinoza, *Tractatus theologico-politicus*, vertaling Frans Akkerman (Darmstadt, Wissenschaftliche Buchgesellschaft, 1979), p. 466).

16. Philip Ball, 'Moore's Law Is Not Just for Computers', Nature Publishing Group, March 2013. http://www.nature.com/news/moore-s-law-is-not-just-for-computers-1.12548

17. Emily Elert, 'Tech Trajectories: Four More Moore's Laws', *ieee Spectrum*, 26 July 2013. http://spectrum.ieee.org/at-work/innovation/tech-trajectories-four-more-moores-laws

18. Peter Marsh, 'The World Struggles to Keep up with the Pace of Change in Science and Technology', *The Financial Times*, 17 June 2014. https://www.ft.com/content/b1da2ef0-eccd-11e3-a57e-00144feabdc0

19. Alan Emery, 'Exponential Population Growth', Kivu. com, May 2014. www.kivu.com/exponential-population-growth/

20. Ray Kurzweil, 'The Law of Accelerating Returns', 2001. www. kurzweilai.net/the-law-of-accelerating-returns

21. Isaac Asimov, *I, Robot* (New York: Bantam, Spectra, 1942).

22. 'ibm's Watson in Africa to Help Solve Problems', bbc News Magazine, 6 February 2014. http://www.bbc.com/news/technology-26065991

23. Ibid.

24. Richard Waters, 'Technology: Rise of the Replicants', *The Financial Times*, March 2014.

25. Daniela Hernandez, 'ibm reveals "brain-like" chip with 4,096 cores', wired.co.uk, 8 August 2014. http://www.wired.co.uk/article/ibm-brain-like-chip

26. Annalee Newitz, 'The First Person in the World to Become a Government-Recognized Cyborg', Rubicon Project, 2 December 2013. http://io9.gizmodo.com/the-first-person-in-the-world-to-become-a-government-re-1474975237

27. Erik Brynjolfsson & Andrew McAfee, *The Second Machine Age* (New York: Norton, 2014).

28. Anjana Ahuja, 'Thinking Machines Are Ripe for a World Takeover', *The Financial Times*, 10 June 2014. https://www.ft.com/content/501be618-efcf-11e3-9b4c-00144feabdc0

29. Erez Aiden & Jean-Baptiste Michel, *Uncharted: Big Data as a Lens on Human Culture* (New York: Riverhead, 2013).

30. Clayton M. Christensen, *The Innovator's Dilemma: When New Technologies Cause Great Firms to Fail* (Boston: Harvard Business Review Press, 2013).

31. Ibid.

32. James Manyika et al., 'Disruptive Technologies: Advances That Will Transform Life, Business, and the Global Economy' (McKinsey Global Institute, May 2013). http://www.mckinsey.com/business-functions/digital-mckinsey/our-insights/disruptive-technologies
33. Ibid.

Chapter 3

34. Andrew Hill, 'Divisions Emerge over Effect of Digital Disruption', *The Financial Times*, 24 January 2014. https://www.ft.com/content/3a7190a2-84df-11e3-8968-00144feab7de
35. 'How Far Can Amazon Go?' *The Economist*, 19 June 2014. http://www.economist.com/news/leaders/21604550-it-has-upended-industries-and-changed-way-world-shops-it-should-beware-abusing
36. 'Amazon's Kindle Swindle', Defective by Design. http://www.defectivebydesign.org
37. Leo Mirani & Max Nisen, 'The Nine Companies That Know More about You than Google or Facebook', *Quartz*, May 2014. https://qz.com/213900/the-nine-companies-that-know-more-about-you-than-google-or-facebook/
38. Natasha Singer, 'A Data Broker Offers a Peek Behind the Curtain', *The New York Times*, 31 August 2013. http://www.nytimes.com/2013/09/01/business/a-data-broker-offers-a-peek-behind-the-curtain.html
39. Eric Siegel, *Predictive Analytics: The Power to Predict Who Will Click, Buy, Lie, or Die* (Hoboken: Wiley, 2013).
40. Michael Persson, 'Data zijn de nieuwe olie', *de Volkskrant*, 26 October 2013. http://www.volkskrant.nl/archief/data-zijn-de-nieuwe-olie~a3533494/
41. World Economic Forum, 'Big Data, Big Impact: New Possibilities for International Development' (Genève: World Economic Forum, undated). http://www3.weforum.org/docs/WEF_TC_MFS_BigDataBigImpact_Briefing_2012.pdf
42. Richard Waters, 'Cloud Price War Is Bad News for Technology Industry's Old Guard', *The Financial Times*, 4

December 2013. https://www.ft.com/content/abdb667a-
5cbf-11e3-a558-00144feabdc0

43. Richard Waters, 'Data Open Doors to Financial
     Innovation', *The Financial Times,* 13 December 2012.
     https://www.ft.com/content/3c59d58a-43fb-11e2-844c-
     00144feabdc0

44. Francisco González, 'Banks Need to Take on Amazon and
     Google or Die', *The Financial Times,* 2 December 2013.
     https://www.ft.com/content/bc70c9fe-4e1d-11e3-8fa5-
     00144feabdc0

45. Quentin Hardy, 'IBM to Announce More Powerful Watson
     via the Internet', *The New York Times,* 14 November 2013.
     http://www.nytimes.com/2013/11/14/technology/IBM-to-
     announce-more-powerful-watson-via-the-internet.html

46. Francisco González, 'Banks Need to Take on Amazon and
     Google or Die', *The Financial Times,* 2 December 2013.
     https://www.ft.com/content/bc70c9fe-4e1d-11e3-8fa5-
     00144feabdc0

47. Tom Whipple, 'Slaves to the Algorithm', *The Economist,*
     June 2013. https://www.1843magazine.com/content/
     features/anonymous/slaves-algorithm

48. Tom Whipple, 'Slaves to the Algorithm', *The Economist,*
     June 2013. https://www.1843magazine.com/content/
     features/anonymous/slaves-algorithm

49. Aaron Tilley, 'Google Acquires Smart Thermostat Maker
     Nest For $3.2 Billion', *Forbes,* 13 January 2014. http://www.
     forbes.com/sites/aarontilley/2014/01/13/google-acquires-
     nest-for-3-2-billion/#39d2b6ac1416

50. 'Big Data at the Speed of Business', undated. http://www-
     01.IBM.com

51. 'Big Data and Apache Hadoop for Oil and Gas', undated.
     http://www.

52. mapr.com

53. Natasha Singer, 'In a Scoreboard of Words, a Cultural
     Guide', *The New York Times,* 7 December 2013. http://www.
     nytimes.com/2013/12/08/technology/in-a-scoreboard-of-
     words-a-cultural-guide.html

54.   Eric Savitz, 'The New Factors Of Production and the Rise of Data-Driven Applications', *Forbes*, 31 October 2011. http://www.forbes.com/sites/ciocentral/2011/10/31/the-new-factors-of-production-and-the-rise-of-data-driven-applications/#471e68b87881

55.   M. Jongsma, 'Analisten voorspellen nog slechter dan het toeval', *Het Financieele Dagblad*, 29 October 2013. https://fd.nl/frontpage/mensen/626140/analisten-voorspellen-nog-slechter-dan-het-toeval

56.   Erez Aiden & Jean-Baptiste Michel, *Uncharted: Big Data as a Lens on Human Culture* (New York: Riverhead, 2013).

57.   Maija Palmer, 'Data Mining Offers Rich Seam', *The Financial Times*, 18 February 2013. https://www.ft.com/content/61c4c378-60bd-11e2-a31a-00144feab49a

58.   Jaron Lanier, *Who Owns the Future?* (London: Penguin Books, 2014).

59.   Marc Hijink, 'Big Blue in Big Data', NRC *Handelsblad*, 15 December 2012. https://www.nrc.nl/nieuws/2012/12/15/big-blue-in-big-data-12591304-a1387820

Chapter 4

60.   Jeremy Bentham, 'Panopticon: The Inspection-House', The Panopticon Writings, 16 June 2001. http://cartome.org/panopticon2.htm

61.   Zygmunt Bauman, *Liquid Modernity* (Cambridge: Polity Press, 2000).

62.   Zygmunt Bauman, *Liquid Modernity* (Cambridge: Polity Press, 2000).

63.   Thomas Mathiesen, *The Viewer Society* (Oslo: University of Oslo, 1997).

64.   Yong-Yeol Ahn, James P. Bagrow & Sune Lehmann, 'Link Communities Reveal Multiscale Complexity in Networks', *Nature* 466 (August 2010), 761-764.

65.   Zygmunt Bauman, *Liquid Modernity* (Cambridge: Polity Press, 2000).

66.   'Viewpoint: Manuel Castells on the Rise of Alternative Economic Cultures', BBC *News Business*, 31 October 2012. http://www.bbc.com/news/business-20027044

67. Zygmunt Bauman, *Liquid Modernity* (Cambridge: Polity Press, 2000).

68. Dave Eggers, *The Circle* (New York: Vintage Books, 2014).

69. Javier Blas & Patrick Jenkins, 'Africa Offers Growth Potential on a Vast Scale', *The Financial Times,* 15 December 2013. https://www.ft.com/content/fa46d61c-574e-11e3-9624-00144feabdc0

70. 'The Holes in Holacracy', *The Economist,* 3 July 2014. http://www.economist.com/news/business/21606267-latest-big-idea-management-deserves-some-scepticism-holes-holacracy

Chapter 5

71. Peter Sloterdijk, *You Must Change Your Life,* translation by Wieland Hoban (Cambridge: Polity Press, 2013)

72. Peter Sloterdijk, *You Must Change Your Life,* translation by Wieland Hoban (Cambridge: Polity Press, 2013).

73. Nikhil Goyal, *One Size Does Not Fit All: a student's assessment of school* (Roslyn Heights: Alternative Education Resource Organisation, 2012).

Chapter 6

74. Lucebert, *Verzamelde Gedichten* (Amsterdam: De Bezige Bij, 2002).

75. Jessica Winch, '10 Well-paid Jobs of the Future', Telegraph, 25 February 2013. http://www.telegraph.co.uk/finance/personalfinance/9892011/10-well-paid-jobs-of-the-future.html

76. Gie Goris & Saskia Sassen, 'Saskia Sassen: "Wij zijn de scheppers van onze eigen toekomst"', www.mo.be, March 2015.

77. Gie Goris & Saskia Sassen, 'Saskia Sassen: "Wij zijn de scheppers van onze eigen toekomst"', www.mo.be, March 2015.

78. David Leonhardt & Kevin Quealy, 'The American Middle Class Is No Longer the World's Richest', *The New York Times,* 22 April 2014. https://www.nytimes.

com/2014/04/23/upshot/the-american-middle-class-is-no-longer-the-worlds-richest.html?_r=0

79. Josefine Ulbrich, 'Who Are the "Middle"? The Struggle of the European Middle Class to Improve Their Living Standards', thebrokeronline.eu, 28 April 2015.

80. Frans Blom, 'Erosie van de middenklasse dwingt tot drastisch verlagen van belasting op arbeid', *Het Financieele Dagblad,* 3 October 2014.

81. Marianne Cooper, 'How the Middle Class Got Screwed: College Costs, Globalization and Our New Insecurity Economy', Salon.com, 2 August 2014.

82. Marianne Cooper, 'How the Middle Class Got Screwed: College Costs, Globalization and Our New Insecurity Economy', Salon.com, 2 August 2014.

83. Frans Blom, 'Erosie van de middenklasse dwingt tot drastisch verlagen van belasting op arbeid', *Het Financieele Dagblad,* 3 October 2014. https://fd.nl/frontpage/economie-politiek/896870/erosie-van-de-middenklasse-dwingt-tot-drastisch-verlagen-van-belasting-op-arbeid

84. Erik Brynjolfsson & Andrew McAfee, *The Second Machine Age* (New York: Norton, 2014).

85. 'Little Things That Mean a Lot', *The Economist,* 9 July 2014. http://www.economist.com/news/business/21607816-businesses-should-aim-lots-small-wins-big-data-add-up-something-big-little

86. Erik Brynjolfsson & Andrew McAfee, *The Second Machine Age* (New York: Norton, 2014).

87. Carl Benedikt Frey & Michael Osborne, 'The Future of Employment: How Susceptible Are Jobs to Computerisation?' Oxford Martin School 2013. http://www.oxfordmartin.ox.ac.uk

88. Maarten Goos & Alan Manning, 'Lousy and Lovely Jobs: The Rising Polarization of Work in Britain', December 2003. http://lse.ac.uk

89. Maarten Goos, Alan Manning & Anna Salomons, 'Explaining Job Polarization: Routine-Biased Technological Change and Offshoring', *The American Economic Review* 104.8 (2014): 2509-2526.

90. 'Deep Knowledge Ventures Appoints Intelligent Investment Analysis Software vital as Board Member', 13 May 2014. prweb.com

91. Jaron Lanier, *Who Owns the Future?* (London: Penguin Books, 2014), p.115

92. Jouke van Dijk & Wim van de Pol, 'Al die verdwenen mbobanen komen dus nooit meer terug', *NRC Handelsblad*, 17 May 2014.

93. Jaron Lanier, *Who Owns the Future?* (London: Penguin Books, 2014).

94. Jaron Lanier, *Who Owns the Future?* (London: Penguin Books, 2014).

95. See also: 'Het reisbureau komt nu ook gewoon thuis', *Algemeen Dagblad,* 12 August 2008.

96. Liesbeth van Tongeren & Pepijn Vloemans, 'Het belasten van zelf opgewekte stroom slaat nergens op', *NRC Handelsblad,* 8 June 2013. https://www.nrc.nl/ nieuws/2013/06/08/het-belasten-van-zelf-opgewekte-stroom-slaat-nergens-12667409-a1368909

97. Jeroen Piersma, 'Abonnement in plaats van uurtarief', *fd Outlook,* 19 December 2014.

98. Andrew Haldane, 'How Low Can You Go?', speech on 18 September 2015. http://bankofengland.co.uk

Chapter 7

99. Zygmunt Bauman, *Liquid Modernity* (Cambridge: Polity Press, 2000).

100. Jeremy Rifkin, *The Zero Marginal Cost Society: The Internet of Things, the Collaborative Commons, and the Eclipse of Capitalism* (New York: Palgrave Macmillan, 2014).

101. Jeremy Rifkin, *The Zero Marginal Cost Society: The Internet of Things, the Collaborative Commons, and the Eclipse of Capitalism* (New York: Palgrave Macmillan, 2014).

102. Jeremy Rifkin, *The Zero Marginal Cost Society: The Internet of Things, the Collaborative Commons, and the Eclipse of Capitalism* (New York: Palgrave Macmillan, 2014).

103. Jeremy Rifkin, *The Zero Marginal Cost Society: The Internet of Things, the Collaborative Commons, and the Eclipse of Capitalism* (New York: Palgrave Macmillan, 2014).

104. John Rawls, *A Theory of Justice*, original edition (Cambridge: Belknap Press, 2005).

105. David Rothkopf, 'Disconnected: As Technological Development Shifts Into Hyperspeed, Governments Remain Stuck in Neutral', *Foreign Policy*, 17 March 2014. http://foreignpolicy.com/2014/03/17/disconnected/

106. Libby Brooks, 'Nicola Sturgeon Calls for Scottish Veto on EU Referendum', *The Guardian*, 29 October 2014. https://www.theguardian.com/politics/2014/oct/29/nicola-sturgeon-scottish-veto-eu-referendum

107. Arif Naqvi, 'Cities, Not Countries, Are the Key to Tomorrow's Economies', *The Financial Times*, 25 April 2014. https://www.ft.com/content/0221bb6e-cb9d-11e3-8ccf-00144feabdco

108. Jonathan Derbyshire, 'If Mayors Ruled the World: A Conversation with Benjamin Barber', *Prospect*, 22 November 2013. http://www.prospectmagazine.co.uk/blogs/jonathan-derbyshire/if-mayors-ruled-the-world-a-conversation-with-benjamin-barber

109. Jonathan Derbyshire, 'If Mayors Ruled the World: A Conversation with Benjamin Barber', *Prospect*, 22 November 2013. http://www.prospectmagazine.co.uk/blogs/jonathan-derbyshire/if-mayors-ruled-the-world-a-conversation-with-benjamin-barber

110. 'Something to Stand on', *The Economist*, 18 January 2014. http://www.economist.com/news/special-report/21593583-proliferating-digital-platforms-will-be-heart-tomorrows-economy-and-even

111. 'Something to Stand on', *The Economist*, 18 January 2014. http://www.economist.com/news/special-report/21593583-proliferating-digital-platforms-will-be-heart-tomorrows-economy-and-even

112. Peter Sloterdijk, *You Must Change Your Life*, translation by Wieland Hoban (Cambridge: Polity Press, 2013

113. Anna Luyten, 'Peter Sloterdijk: "Ik zeg u: de crisis zal een nieuwe elite brengen"', *Vrij Nederland,* 6 June 2009. https://www.vn.nl/peter-sloterdijk-ik-zeg-u-de-crisis-zal-een-nieuwe-elite-brengen/

Chapter 8

114. Henry Mintzberg, *Structure in Fives: Designing Effective Organizations* (Englewood Cliffs: Prentice-Hall, 1983).
115. Henry Mintzberg, *Structure in Fives: Designing Effective Organizations* (Englewood Cliffs: Prentice-Hall, 1983).
116. Henry Mintzberg, *Structure in Fives: Designing Effective Organizations* (Englewood Cliffs: Prentice-Hall, 1983).
117. http://blog.dilbert.com/post/102964898391/the-future-ofmiddle-management
118. Lynda Gratton, 'Column: The End of the Middle Manager', Harvard Business Publishing, January 2011. http://hbr.org
119. Henry Mintzberg, 'Why do we say "Top Management" yet never "Bottom Management"?', blog dated 19 March 2015 on http://www.mintzberg.org
120. Ikujirõ Nonaka, Ryoko Toyama & Toru Hirata, *Managing Flow: A Process Theory of the Knowledge-Based Firm* (New York: Palgrave Macmillan, 2008).
121. 'Facebook Paid £4,327 Corporation Tax In 2014', 12 October 2015. , bbc.co.uk
122. Taxpolicycenter.org
123. Robert Putnam, *Bowling Alone* (New York: Simon & Schuster, 2001).
124. Michael Schudson, 'The Varieties of Civic Experience', *Citizenship Studies* vol. 10 no. 5 (November 2006), pp. 591-606.

Tot slot

125. http://www.john-uebersax.com/plato/myths/protagoras.htm
126. Michel de Montaigne, *Essays* (NuVision Publications, 2007).
127. Michel de Montaigne, *Essays* (NuVision Publications, 2007).

Index

www.ingramcontent.com/pod-product-compliance
Lightning Source LLC
Chambersburg PA
CBHW070908270326
41927CB00011B/2494

9789492004420